SYNTACTIC STRUCTURES

JANUA LINGUARUM

STUDIA MEMORIAE
NICOLAI VAN WIJK DEDICATA

edenda curat

C. H. VAN SCHOONEVELD
INDIANA UNIVERSITY

SERIES MINOR
NR. 4

1957

MOUTON
THE HAGUE · PARIS

SYNTACTIC STRUCTURES

by

NOAM CHOMSKY

MASSACHUSETTS INSTITUTE OF TECHNOLOGY

MOUTON PUBLISHERS · THE HAGUE · PARIS

First printing 1957

Second printing 1962

Third printing 1963

Fourth printing 1964

Fifth printing 1965

Sixth printing 1966

Seventh printing 1968

Eighth printing 1969

Ninth printing 1971

Tenth printing 1972

Eleventh printing 1975

Twelfth printing 1976

Thirteenth printing 1978

Fourteenth printing 1985

ISBN 90 279 3385 5

Printed on acid free paper

Printing: Kupijai & Prochnow, Berlin. – Binding: Dieter Mikolai, Berlin.
Printed in Germany.

PREFACE

This study deals with syntactic structure both in the broad sense (as opposed to semantics) and the narrow sense (as opposed to phonemics and morphology). It forms part of an attempt to construct a formalized general theory of linguistic structure and to explore the foundations of such a theory. The search for rigorous formulation in linguistics has a much more serious motivation than mere concern for logical niceties or the desire to purify well-established methods of linguistic analysis. Precisely constructed models for linguistic structure can play an important role, both negative and positive, in the process of discovery itself. By pushing a precise but inadequate formulation to an unacceptable conclusion, we can often expose the exact source of this inadequacy and, consequently, gain a deeper understanding of the linguistic data. More positively, a formalized theory may automatically provide solutions for many problems other than those for which it was explicitly designed. Obscure and intuition-bound notions can neither lead to absurd conclusions nor provide new and correct ones, and hence they fail to be useful in two important respects. I think that some of those linguists who have questioned the value of precise and technical development of linguistic theory may have failed to recognize the productive potential in the method of rigorously stating a proposed theory and applying it strictly to linguistic material with no attempt to avoid unacceptable conclusions by *ad hoc* adjustments or loose formulation. The results reported below were obtained by a conscious attempt to follow this course systematically. Since this fact may be obscured by the informality of the presentation, it is important to emphasize it here.

Specifically, we shall investigate three models for linguistic structure and seek to determine their limitations. We shall find that a certain very simple communication theoretic model of language and a more powerful model that incorporates a large part of what is now generally known as "immediate constituent analysis" cannot properly serve the purposes of grammatical description. The investigation and application of these models brings to light certain facts about linguistic structure and exposes several gaps in linguistic theory; in particular, a failure to account for such relations between sentences as the active-passive relation. We develop a third, *transformational* model for linguistic structure which is more powerful than the immediate constituent model in certain important respects and which does account for such relations in a natural way. When we formulate the theory of transformations carefully and apply it freely to English, we find that it provides a good deal of insight into a wide range of phenomena beyond those for which it was specifically designed. In short, we find that formalization can, in fact, perform both the negative and the positive service commented on above.

During the entire period of this research I have had the benefit of very frequent and lengthy discussions with Zellig S. Harris. So many of his ideas and suggestions are incorporated in the text below and in the research on which it is based that I will make no attempt to indicate them by special reference. Harris' work on transformational structure, which proceeds from a somewhat different point of view from that taken below, is developed in items 15, 16, and 19 of the bibliography (p. 115). In less obvious ways, perhaps, the course of this research has been influenced strongly by the work of Nelson Goodman and W. V. Quine. I have discussed most of this material at length with Morris Halle, and have benefited very greatly from his comments and suggestions. Eric Lenneberg, Israel Scheffler, and Yehoshua Bar-Hillel have read earlier versions of this manuscript and have made many valuable criticisms and suggestions on presentation and content.

The work on the theory of transformations and the transformational structure of English which, though only briefly sketched below, serves as the basis for much of the discussion, was largely carried out in 1951 – 55 while I was a Junior Fellow of the Society of Fellows, Harvard University. I would like to express my gratitude to the Society of Fellows for having provided me with the freedom to carry on this research.

This work was supported in part by the U.S.A. Army (Signal Corps), the Air Force (Office of Scientific Research, Air Research and Development Command), and the Navy (Office of Naval Research); and in part by the National Science Foundation and the Eastman Kodak Corporation.

Massachusetts Institute of Technology,   NOAM CHOMSKY
Department of Modern Languages and
Research Laboratory of Electronics,
Cambridge, Mass.

August 1, 1956.

TABLE OF CONTENTS

1

INTRODUCTION

Syntax is the study of the principles and processes by which sentences are constructed in particular languages. Syntactic investigation of a given language has as its goal the construction of a grammar that can be viewed as a device of some sort for producing the sentences of the language under analysis. More generally, linguists must be concerned with the problem of determining the fundamental underlying properties of successful grammars. The ultimate outcome of these investigations should be a theory of linguistic structure in which the descriptive devices utilized in particular grammars are presented and studied abstractly, with no specific reference to particular languages. One function of this theory is to provide a general method for selecting a grammar for each language, given a corpus of sentences of this language.

The central notion in linguistic theory is that of "linguistic level." A linguistic level, such as phonemics, morphology, phrase structure, is essentially a set of descriptive devices that are made available for the construction of grammars; it constitutes a certain method for representing utterances. We can determine the adequacy of a linguistic theory by developing rigorously and precisely the form of grammar corresponding to the set of levels contained within this theory, and then investigating the possibility of constructing simple and revealing grammars of this form for natural languages. We shall study several different conceptions of linguistic structure in this manner, considering a succession of linguistic levels of increasing complexity which correspond to more and more powerful modes of grammatical description; and we shall attempt to show that linguistic theory must contain at least these levels if it is to provide, in particular, a satisfactory grammar of English. Finally, we shall suggest that this purely formal investigation of the structure of language has certain interesting implications for semantic studies.[1]

---

[1] The motivation for the particular orientation of the research reported here is discussed below in § 6.

2

THE INDEPENDENCE OF GRAMMAR

2.1 From now on I will consider a *language* to be a set (finite or infinite) of sentences, each finite in length and constructed out of a finite set of elements. All natural languages in their spoken or written form are languages in this sense, since each natural language has a finite number of phonemes (or letters in its alphabet) and each sentence is representable as a finite sequence of these phonemes (or letters), though there are infinitely many sentences. Similarly, the set of 'sentences' of some formalized system of mathematics can be considered a language. The fundamental aim in the linguistic analysis of a language L is to separate the *grammatical* sequences which are the sentences of L from the *ungrammatical* sequences which are not sentences of L and to study the structure of the grammatical sequences. The grammar of L will thus be a device that generates all of the grammatical sequences of L and none of the ungrammatical ones. One way to test the adequacy of a grammar proposed for L is to determine whether or not the sequences that it generates are actually grammatical, i.e., acceptable to a native speaker, etc. We can take certain steps towards providing a behavioral criterion for grammaticalness so that this test of adequacy can be carried out. For the purposes of this discussion, however, suppose that we assume intuitive knowledge of the grammatical sentences of English and ask what sort of grammar will be able to do the job of producing these in some effective and illuminating way. We thus face a familiar task of explication of some intuitive concept — in this case, the concept "grammatical in English," and more generally, the concept "grammatical."

Notice that in order to set the aims of grammar significantly it is sufficient to assume a partial knowledge of sentences and non-sentences. That is, we may assume for this discussion that certain sequences of phonemes are definitely sentences, and that certain other sequences are definitely non-sentences. In many intermediate cases we shall be prepared to let the grammar itself decide, when the grammar is set up in the simplest way so that it includes the clear sentences and excludes the clear non-sentences. This is a familiar feature of explication.[1] A certain number of clear cases, then, will provide us with a criterion of adequacy for any particular grammar. For a single language, taken in isolation, this provides only a weak test of adequacy, since many different grammars may handle the clear cases properly. This can be generalized to a very strong condition, however, if we insist that the clear cases be handled properly for *each* language by grammars all of which are constructed by the same method. That is, each grammar is related to the corpus of sentences in the language it describes in a way fixed in advance for all grammars by a given linguistic theory. We then have a very strong test of adequacy for a linguistic theory that attemps to give a general explanation for the notion "grammatical sentence" in terms of "observed sentence," and for the set of grammars constructed in accordance with such a theory. It is furthermore a reasonable requirement, since we are interested not only in particular languages, but also in the general nature of Language. There is a great deal more that can be said about this crucial topic, but this would take us too far afield. Cf. § 6.

2.2   On what basis do we actually go about separating grammatical sequences from ungrammatical sequences? I shall not attempt to

---

[1]   Cf., for example, N. Goodman, *The structure of appearance* (Cambridge, 1951), pp. 5–6. Notice that to meet the aims of grammar, given a linguistic theory, it is sufficient to have a partial knowledge of the sentences (i.e., a corpus) of the language, since a linguistic theory will state the relation between the set of observed sentences and the set of grammatical sentences; i.e., it will define "grammatical sentence" in terms of "observed sentence," certain properties of the observed sentences, and certain properties of grammars. To use Quine's formulation, a linguistic theory will give a general explanation for what 'could' be in language on the basis of "what *is* plus *simplicity* of the laws whereby we describe and extrapolate what is". (W. V. Quine, *From a logical point of view* [Cambridge, 1953], p. 54). Cf. § 6.1.

give a complete answer to this question here (cf. §§ 6.7), but I would like to point out that several answers that immediately suggest themselves could not be correct. First, it is obvious that the set of grammatical sentences cannot be identified with any particular corpus of utterances obtained by the linguist in his field work. Any grammar of a language will *project* the finite and somewhat accidental corpus of observed utterances to a set (presumably infinite) of grammatical utterances. In this respect, a grammar mirrors the behavior of the speaker who, on the basis of a finite and accidental experience with language, can produce or understand an indefinite number of new sentences. Indeed, any explication of the notion "grammatical in L" (i.e., any characterization of "grammatical in L" in terms of "observed utterance of L") can be thought of as offering an explanation for this fundamental aspect of linguistic behavior.

2.3 Second, the notion "grammatical" cannot be identified with "meaningful" or "significant" in any semantic sense. Sentences (1) and (2) are equally nonsensical, but any speaker of English will recognize that only the former is grammatical.

(1) Colorless green ideas sleep furiously.

(2) Furiously sleep ideas green colorless.

Similarly, there is no semantic reason to prefer (3) to (5) or (4) to (6), but only (3) and (4) are grammatical sentences of English.

(3) have you a book on modern music?

(4) the book seems interesting.

(5) read you a book on modern music?

(6) the child seems sleeping.

Such examples suggest that any search for a semantically based definition of "grammaticalness" will be futile. We shall see, in fact, in § 7, that there are deep structural reasons for distinguishing (3) and (4) from (5) and (6); but before we are able to find an explanation for such facts as these we shall have to carry the theory of syntactic structure a good deal beyond its familiar limits.

2.4 Third, the notion "grammatical in English" cannot be identified in any way with the notion "high order of statistical approximation to English." It is fair to assume that neither sentence (1) nor (2) (nor indeed any part of these sentences) has ever occurred in an English discourse. Hence, in any statistical model for grammaticalness, these sentences will be ruled out on identical grounds as equally 'remote' from English. Yet (1), though nonsensical, is grammatical, while (2) is not. Presented with these sentences, a speaker of English will read (1) with a normal sentence intonation, but he will read (2) with a falling intonation on each word; in fact, with just the intonation pattern given to any sequence of unrelated words. He treats each word in (2) as a separate phrase. Similarly, he will be able to recall (1) much more easily than (2), to learn it much more quickly, etc. Yet he may never have heard or seen any pair of words from these sentences joined in actual discourse. To choose another example, in the context "I saw a fragile—," the words "whale" and "of" may have equal (i.e., zero) frequency in the past linguistic experience of a speaker who will immediately recognize that one of these substitutions, but not the other, gives a grammatical sentence. We cannot, of course, appeal to the fact that sentences such as (1) 'might' be uttered in some sufficiently far-fetched context, while (2) would never be, since the basis for this differentiation between (1) and (2) is precisely what we are interested in determining.

Evidently, one's ability to produce and recognize grammatical utterances is not based on notions of statistical approximation and the like. The custom of calling grammatical sentences those that "can occur", or those that are "possible", has been responsible for some confusion here. It is natural to understand "possible" as meaning "highly probable" and to assume that the linguist's sharp distinction between grammatical and ungrammatical[2] is motivated by a feeling that since the 'reality' of language is too complex to be described completely, he must content himself with a schematized

---

[2] Below we shall suggest that this sharp distinction may be modified in favor of a notion of levels of grammaticalness. But this has no bearing on the point at issue here. Thus (1) and (2) will be at different levels of grammaticalness even if (1) is assigned a lower degree of grammaticalness than, say, (3) and (4); but they will be at the same level of statistical remoteness from English. The same is true of an indefinite number of similar pairs.

version replacing "zero probability, and all extremely low probabilities, by *impossible*, and all higher probabilities by *possible*."[3] We see, however, that this idea is quite incorrect, and that a structural analysis cannot be understood as a schematic summary developed by sharpening the blurred edges in the full statistical picture. If we rank the sequences of a given length in order of statistical approximation to English, we will find both grammatical and ungrammatical sequences scattered throughout the list; there appears to be no particular relation between order of approximation and grammaticalness. Despite the undeniable interest and importance of semantic and statistical studies of language, they appear to have no direct relevance to the problem of determining or characterizing the set of grammatical utterances. I think that we are forced to conclude that grammar is autonomous and independent of meaning, and that probabilistic models give no particular insight into some of the basic problems of syntactic structure.[4]

---

[3] C. F. Hockett, *A manual of phonology* (Baltimore, 1955), p. 10.

[4] We return to the question of the relation between semantics and syntax in §§ 8, 9, where we argue that this relation can only be studied after the syntactic structure has been determined on independent grounds. I think that much the same thing is true of the relation between syntactic and statistical studies of language. Given the grammar of a language, one can study the use of the language statistically in various ways; and the development of probabilistic models for the use of language (as distinct from the syntactic structure of language) can be quite rewarding. Cf. B. Mandelbrot, "Structure formelle des textes et communication: deux études," *Word* 10.1–27 (1954); H. A. Simon, "On a class of skew distribution functions," *Biometrika* 42.425–40 (1955).

One might seek to develop a more elaborate relation between statistical and syntactic structure than the simple order of approximation model we have rejected. I would certainly not care to argue that any such relation is unthinkable, but I know of no suggestion to this effect that does not have obvious flaws. Notice, in particular, that for any *n*, we can find a string whose first *n* words may occur as the beginning of a grammatical sentence S_1 and whose last *n* words may occur as the ending of some grammatical sentence S_2, but where S_1 must be distinct from S_2. For example, consider the sequences of the form "the man who ... are here," where ... may be a verb phrase of arbitrary length. Notice also that we can have new but perfectly grammatical sequences of word classes, e.g., a sequence of adjectives longer than any ever before produced in the context "I saw a — house." Various attempts to explain the grammatical-ungrammatical distinction, as in the case of (1), (2), on the basis of frequency of sentence type, order of approximation of word class sequences, etc., will run afoul of numerous facts like these.

3

AN ELEMENTARY LINGUISTIC THEORY

3.1 Assuming the set of grammatical sentences of English to be given, we now ask what sort of device can produce this set (equivalently, what sort of theory gives an adequate account of the structure of this set of utterances). We can think of each sentence of this set as a sequence of phonemes of finite length. A language is an enormously involved system, and it is quite obvious that any attempt to present directly the set of grammatical phoneme sequences would lead to a grammar so complex that it would be practically useless. For this reason (among others), linguistic description proceeds in terms of a system of "levels of representations." Instead of stating the phonemic structure of sentences directly, the linguist sets up such 'higher level' elements as morphemes, and states separately the morphemic structure of sentences and the phonemic structure of morphemes. It can easily be seen that the joint description of these two levels will be much simpler than a direct description of the phonemic structure of sentences.

Let us now consider various ways of describing the morphemic structure of sentences. We ask what sort of grammar is necessary to generate all the sequences of morphemes (or words) that constitute grammatical English sentences, and only these.

One requirement that a grammar must certainly meet is that it be finite. Hence the grammar cannot simply be a list of all morpheme (or word) sequences, since there are infinitely many of these. A familiar communication theoretic model for language suggests a way out of this difficulty. Suppose that we have a machine that can be in any one of a finite number of different internal states, and suppose that this machine switches from one state to another by producing a certain symbol (let us say, an English word). One of these states is an *initial state*; another is a *final state*. Suppose that the machine begins in the initial state, runs through a sequence of states (producing a word with each transition), and ends in the final state. Then we call the sequence of words that has been produced a "sentence". Each such machine thus defines a certain language; namely, the set of sentences that can be produced in this way. Any language that can be produced by a machine of this sort we call a *finite state language*; and we can call the machine itself a *finite state grammar*. A finite state grammar can be represented graphically in the form of a "state diagram".[1] For example, the grammar that produces just the two sentences "the man comes" and "the men come" can be represented by the following state diagram:

(7)

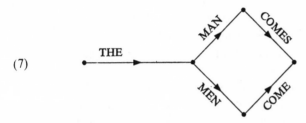

We can extend this grammar to produce an infinite number of sentences by adding closed loops. Thus the finite grammar of the subpart of English containing the above sentences in addition to "the old man comes", "the old old man comes", ..., "the old men come", "the old old men come", ..., can be represented by the following state diagram:

(8)

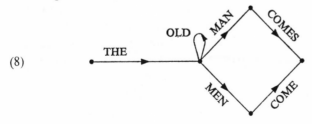

[1] C. E. Shannon and W. Weaver, *The mathematical theory of communication* (Urbana, 1949), pp. 15f.

Given a state diagram, we produce a sentence by tracing a path from the initial point on the left to the final point on the right, always proceeding in the direction of the arrows. Having reached a certain point in the diagram, we can proceed along any path leading from this point, whether or not this path has been traversed before in constructing the sentence in question. Each node in such a diagram thus corresponds to a state of the machine. We can allow transition from one state to another in several ways, and we can have any number of closed loops of any length. The machines that produce languages in this manner are known mathematically as "finite state Markov processes." To complete this elementary communication theoretic model for language, we assign a probability to each transition from state to state. We can then calculate the "uncertainty" associated with each state and we can define the "information content" of the language as the average uncertainty, weighted by the probability of being in the associated states. Since we are studying grammatical, not statistical structure of language here, this generalization does not concern us.

This conception of language is an extremely powerful and general one. If we can adopt it, we can view the speaker as being essentially a machine of the type considered. In producing a sentence, the speaker begins in the initial state, produces the first word of the sentence, thereby switching into a second state which limits the choice of the second word, etc. Each state through which he passes represents the grammatical restrictions that limit the choice of the next word at this point in the utterance.[2]

In view of the generality of this conception of language, and its utility in such related disciplines as communication theory, it is important to inquire into the consequences of adopting this point of view in the syntactic study of some language such as English or a formalized system of mathematics. Any attempt to construct a finite state grammar for English runs into serious difficulties and complications at the very outset, as the reader can easily convince himself. However, it is unnecessary to attempt to show this by

[2]   This is essentially the model of language that Hockett develops in *A manual of phonology* (Baltimore, 1955), 02.

example, in view of the following more general remark about English:

(9)   English is not a finite state language.

That is, it is *impossible*, not just difficult, to construct a device of the type described above (a diagram such as (7) or (8)) which will produce all and only the grammatical sentences of English. To demonstrate (9) it is necessary to define the syntactic properties of English more precisely. We shall proceed to describe certain syntactic properties of English which indicate that, under any reasonable delimitation of the set of sentences of the language, (9) can be regarded as a theorem concerning English. To go back to the question asked in the second paragraph of § 3, (9) asserts that it is not possible to state the morphemic structure of sentences directly by means of some such device as a state diagram, and that the Markov process conception of language outlined above cannot be accepted, at least for the purposes of grammar.

3.2   A language is defined by giving its 'alphabet' (i.e., the finite set of symbols out of which its sentences are constructed) and its grammatical sentences. Before investigating English directly, let us consider several languages whose alphabets contain just the letters a, b, and whose sentences are as defined in (10i–iii):

(10) (i)   *ab, aabb, aaabbb*, ..., and in general, all sentences consisting of n occurrences of a followed by n occurrences of b and only these;

    (ii)   *aa, bb, abba, baab, aaaa, bbbb, aabbaa, abbbba*, ..., and in general, all sentences consisting of a string X followed by the 'mirror image' of X (i.e., X in reverse), and only these;

    (iii)   *aa, bb, abab, baba, aaaa, bbbb, aabaab, abbabb*, ..., and in general, all sentences consisting of a string X of a's and b's followed by the identical string X, and only these.

We can easily show that each of these three languages is not a finite state language. Similarly, languages such as (10) where the a's and b's in question are not consecutive, but are embedded in other strings, will fail to be finite state languages under quite general conditions.[3]

But it is clear that there are subparts of English with the basic form of (10i) and (10ii). Let $S_1, S_2, S_3, \ldots$ be declarative sentences in English. Then we can have such English sentences as:

(11) (i) If S_1, then S_2.

    (ii) Either S_3, or S_4.

    (iii) The man who said that S_5, is arriving today.

In (11i), we cannot have "or" in place of "then"; in (11ii), we cannot have "then" in place of "or"; in (11iii), we cannot have "are" instead of "is". In each of these cases there is a dependency between words on opposite sides of the comma (i.e., "if"–"then", "either"–"or", "man"–"is"). But between the interdependent words, in each case, we can insert a declarative sentence S_1, S_3, S_5, and this declarative sentence may in fact be one of (11 i–iii). Thus if in (11i) we take S_1 as (11ii) and S_3 as (11iii), we will have the sentence:

(12)   if, either (11iii), or S_4, then S_2,

and S_5 in (11iii) may again be one of the sentences of (11). It is clear, then, that in English we can find a sequence $a + S_1 + b$, where there is a dependency between a and b, and we can select as S_1 another sequence containing $c + S_2 + d$, where there is a dependency between c and d, then select as S_2 another sequence of this form, etc. A set of sentences that is constructed in this way (and we see from (11) that there are several possibilities available for such construction— (11) comes nowhere near exhausting these possibilities) will have all of the mirror image properties of (10ii) which exclude (10ii) from the set of finite state languages. Thus we can find various kinds of non-

---

    ³ See my "Three models for the description of language," *I.R.E. Transactions on Information Theory*, vol. IT-2, Proceedings of the symposium on information theory, Sept., 1956, for a statement of such conditions and a proof of (9). Notice in particular that the set of well-formed formulas of any formalized system of mathematics or logic will fail to constitute a finite state language, because of paired parentheses or equivalent restrictions.

finite state models within English. This is a rough indication of the lines along which a rigorous proof of (9) can be given, on the assumption that such sentences as (11) and (12) belong to English, while sentences that contradict the cited dependencies of (11) (e.g., "either S_1, then S_2," etc.) do not belong to English. Note that many of the sentences of the form (12), etc., will be quite strange and unusual (they can often be made less strange by replacing "if" by "whenever", "on the assumption that", "if it is the case that", etc., without changing the substance of our remarks). But they are all grammatical sentences, formed by processes of sentence construction so simple and elementary that even the most rudimentary English grammar would contain them. They can be understood, and we can even state quite simply the conditions under which they can be true. It is difficult to conceive of any possible motivation for excluding them from the set of grammatical English sentences. Hence it seems quite clear that no theory of linguistic structure based exclusively on Markov process models and the like, will be able to explain or account for the ability of a speaker of English to produce and understand new utterances, while he rejects other new sequences as not belonging to the language.

3.3   We might arbitrarily decree that such processes of sentence formation in English as those we are discussing cannot be carried out more than n times, for some fixed n. This would of course make English a finite state language, as, for example, would a limitation of English sentences to length of less than a million words. Such arbitrary limitations serve no useful purpose, however. The point is that there are processes of sentence formation that finite state grammars are intrinsically not equipped to handle. If these processes have no finite limit, we can prove the literal inapplicability of this elementary theory. If the processes have a limit, then the construction of a finite state grammar will not be literally out of the question, since it will be possible to list the sentences, and a list is essentially a trivial finite state grammar. But this grammar will be so complex that it will be of little use or interest. In general, the assumption that languages are infinite is made in order to simplify the description of these languages. If a grammar does not have recursive devices (closed loops, as in (8), in the finite state grammar) it will be prohibitively complex. If it does have recursive devices of some sort, it will produce infinitely many sentences.

In short, the approach to the analysis of grammaticalness suggested here in terms of a finite state Markov process that produces sentences from left to right, appears to lead to a dead end just as surely as the proposals rejected in § 2. If a grammar of this type produces all English sentences, it will produce many non-sentences as well. If it produces only English sentences, we can be sure that there will be an infinite number of true sentences, false sentences, reasonable questions, etc., which it simply will not produce.

The conception of grammar which has just been rejected represents in a way the minimal linguistic theory that merits serious consideration. A finite state grammar is the simplest type of grammar which, with a finite amount of apparatus, can generate an infinite number of sentences. We have seen that such a limited linguistic theory is not adequate; we are forced to search for some more powerful type of grammar and some more 'abstract' form of linguistic theory. The notion of "linguistic level of representation" put forth at the outset of this section must be modified and elaborated. At least one linguistic level *cannot* have this simple structure. That is, on some level, it will not be the case that each sentence is represented simply as a finite sequence of elements of some sort, generated from left to right by some simple device. Alternatively, we must give up the hope of finding a *finite* set of levels, ordered from high to low, so constructed that we can generate all utterances by stating the permitted sequences of highest level elements, the constituency of each highest level element in terms of elements of the second level, etc., finally stating the phonemic constituency of elements of the next-to-lowest level.[4] At the outset of § 3, we

---

[4] A third alternative would be to retain the notion of a linguistic level as a simple linear method of representation, but to generate at least one such level from left to right by a device with more capacity than a finite state Markov process. There are so many difficulties with the notion of linguistic level based on left to right generation, both in terms of complexity of description and lack

proposed that levels be established in this way in order to *simplify* the description of the set of grammatical phoneme sequences. If a language can be described in an elementary, left-to-right manner in terms of a single level (i.e., if it is a finite state language) then this description may indeed be simplified by construction of such higher levels; but to generate non-finite state languages such as English we need fundamentally different methods, and a more general concept of "linguistic level".

---

of explanatory power (cf. § 8), that it seems pointless to pursue this approach any further. The grammars that we discuss below that do not generate from left to right also correspond to processes less elementary than finite state Markov processes. But they are perhaps less powerful than the kind of device that would be required for direct left-to-right generation of English. Cf. my "Three models for the description of language" for some futher discussion.

4

PHRASE STRUCTURE

4.1 Customarily, linguistic description on the syntactic level is formulated in terms of constituent analysis (parsing). We now ask what form of grammar is presupposed by description of this sort. We find that the new form of grammar is *essentially* more powerful than the finite state model rejected above, and that the associated concept of "linguistic level" is different in fundamental respects.

As a simple example of the new form for grammars associated with constituent analysis, consider the following:

(13) (i)   *Sentence* → *NP* + *VP*
   (ii)   *NP* → *T* + *N*
  (iii)   *VP* → *Verb* + *NP*
  (iv)   *T* → *the*
   (v)   *N* → *man, ball*, etc.
  (vi)   *Verb* → *hit, took*, etc.

Suppose that we interpret each rule *X* → *Y* of (13) as the instruction "rewrite *X* as *Y*". We shall call (14) a *derivation* of the sentence "the man hit the ball." where the numbers at the right of each line of the derivation refer to the rule of the "grammar" (13) used in constructing that line from the preceding line.[1]

---

[1]   The numbered rules of English grammar to which reference will constantly be made in the following pages are collected and properly ordered in § 12, *Appendix II*. The notational conventions that we shall use throughout the discussion of English structure are stated in § 11, *Appendix I*.

In his "Axiomatic syntax: the construction and evaluation of a syntactic calculus," *Language* 31.409–14 (1955), Harwood describes a system of word class analysis similar in form to the system developed below for phrase structure. The system he describes would be concerned only with the relation between $T + N + Verb + T + N$ and *the + man + hit + the + ball* in the example discussed

(14) *Sentence*
    NP + VP   (i)
    T + N + VP   (ii)
    T + N + Verb + NP   (iii)
    the + N + Verb + NP   (iv)
    the + man + Verb + NP   (v)
    the + man + hit + NP   (vi)
    the + man + hit + T + N   (ii)
    the + man + hit + the + N   (iv)
    the + man + hit + the + ball   (v)

Thus the second line of (14) is formed from the first line by rewriting *Sentence* as *NP + VP* in accordance with rule (i) of (13); the third line is formed from the second by rewriting *NP* as *T + N* in accordance with rule (ii) of (13); etc. We can represent the derivation (14) in an obvious way by means of the following diagram:

(15)   *Sentence*

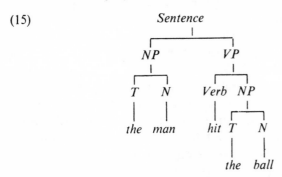

The diagram (15) conveys less information than the derivation (14), since it does not tell us in what order the rules were applied in (14).

in (13)–(15); i.e., the grammar would contain the "initial string" $T + N + Verb + T + N$ and such rules as (13 iv–vi). It would thus be a weaker system than the elementary theory discussed in § 3, since it could not generate an infinite language with a finite grammar. While Harwood's formal account (pp. 409–11) deals only with word class analysis, the linguistic application (p. 412) is a case of immediate constituent analysis, with the classes $C_{i...m}$ presumably taken to be classes of word sequences. This extended application is not quite compatible with the formal account, however. For example, none of the proposed measures of goodness of fit can stand without revision under this reinterpretation of the formalism.

Given (14), we can construct (15) uniquely, but not vice versa, since it is possible to construct a derivation that reduces to (15) with a different order of application of the rules. The diagram (15) retains just what is essential in (14) for the determination of the phrase structure (constituent analysis) of the derived sentence "the man hit the ball." A sequence of words of this sentence is a constituent of type Z if we can trace this sequence back to a single point of origin in (15), and this point of origin is labelled Z. Thus "hit the ball" can be traced back to VP in (15); hence "hit the ball" is a VP in the derived sentence. But "man hit" cannot be traced back to any single point of origin in (15); hence "man hit" is not a constituent at all.

We say that two derivations are *equivalent* if they reduce to the same diagram of the form (15). Occasionally, a grammar may permit us to construct nonequivalent derivations for a given sentence. Under these circumstances, we say that we have a case of "constructional homonymity",[2] and if our grammar is correct, this sentence of the language should be ambiguous. We return to the important notion of constructional homonymity below.

One generalization of (13) is clearly necessary. We must be able to limit application of a rule to a certain context. Thus T can be rewritten a if the following noun is singular, but not if it is plural; similarly, *Verb* can be rewritten "hits" if the preceding noun is *man*, but not if it is *men*. In general, if we wish to limit the rewriting of X as Y to the context $Z - W$, we can state in the grammar the rule

(16) $Z + X + W \rightarrow Z + Y + W$.

For example, in the case of singular and plural verbs, instead of having *Verb* → *hits* as an additional rule of (13), we should have

(17) $NP_{sing} + Verb \rightarrow NP_{sing} + hits$

indicating that *Verb* is rewritten *hits* only in the context $NP_{sing}-$.

---

² See § 8.1 for some examples of constructional homonymity. See my *The logical structure of linguistic theory* (mimeographed); "Three models for the description of language" (above, p. 22, fn. 3); C. F. Hockett, "Two models of grammatical description," *Linguistics Today, Word* 10.210–33 (1954); R. S. Wells, "Immediate constituents," *Language* 23.81–117 (1947) for more detailed discussion.

Correspondingly, (13ii) will have to be restated to include NP_{sing} and NP_{pl}.[3] This is a straightforward generalization of (13). One feature of (13) must be preserved, however, as it is in (17): only a single element can be rewritten in any single rule; i.e., in (16), X must be a single symbol such as T, $Verb$, and not a sequence such as $T + N$. If this condition is not met, we will not be able to recover properly the phrase structure of derived sentences from the associated diagrams of the form (15), as we did above.

We can now describe more generally the form of grammar associated with the theory of linguistic structure based upon constituent analysis. Each such grammar is defined by a finite set Σ of initial strings and a finite set F of 'instruction formulas' of the form $X \rightarrow Y$ in.erpreted: "rewrite X as Y." Though X need not be a single symbol, only a single symbol of X can be rewritten in forming Y. In the grammar (13), the only member of the set Σ of initial strings was the single symbol *Sentence*, and F consisted of the rules (i) – (vi); but we might want to extend Σ to include, for example, *Declarative Sentence*, *Interrogative Sentence*, as additional symbols. Given the grammar [Σ, F], we define a *derivation* as a finite sequence of strings, beginning with an initial string of Σ, and with each string in the sequence being derived from the preceding string by application of one of the instruction formulas of F. Thus (14) is a derivation, and the five-termed sequence of strings consisting of the first five lines of (14) is also a derivation. Certain derivations are *terminated* derivations, in the sense that their final string cannot be rewritten any further by the rules F. Thus (14) is a terminated derivation, but the sequence consisting of the first five

---

[3] Thus in a more complete grammar, (13ii) might be replaced by a set of rules that includes the following:

$$NP \rightarrow \begin{Bmatrix} NP_{sing} \\ NP_{pl} \end{Bmatrix}$$
$$NP_{sing} \rightarrow T + N + \emptyset \; (+ \textit{Prepositional Phrase})$$
$$NP_{pl} \rightarrow T + N + S \; (+ \textit{Prepositional Phrase})$$

where S is the morpheme which is singular for verbs and plural for nouns ("comes," "boys"), and $\emptyset$ is the morpheme which is singular for nouns and plural for verbs ("boy," "come"). We shall omit all mention of first and second person throughout this discussion. Identification of the nominal and verbal number affix is actually of questionable validity.

lines of (14) is not. If a string is the last line of a terminated derivation, we say that it is a *terminal* string. Thus *the + man + hit + the + ball* is a terminal string from the grammar (13). Some grammars of the form [Σ, F] may have no terminal strings, but we are interested only in grammars that do have terminal strings, i.e., that describe some language. A set of strings is called a *terminal language* if it is the set of terminal strings for some grammar [Σ, F]. Thus each such grammar defines some terminal language (perhaps the 'empty' language containing no sentences), and each terminal language is produced by some grammar of the form [Σ, F]. Given a terminal language and its grammar, we can reconstruct the phrase structure of each sentence of the language (each terminal string of the grammar) by considering the associated diagrams of the form (15), as we saw above. We can also define the grammatical relations in these languages in a formal way in terms of the associated diagrams.

4.2   In § 3 we considered languages, called "finite state languages", which were generated by finite state Markov processes. Now we are considering terminal languages that are generated by systems of the form [Σ, F]. These two types of languages are related in the following way

Theorem: Every finite state language is a terminal language, but there are terminal languages which are not finite state languages.[4]

The import of this theorem is that description in terms of phrase structure is essentially more powerful than description in terms of the elementary theory presented above in § 3. As examples of terminal languages that are not finite state languages we have the languages (10i), (10ii) discussed in § 3. Thus the language (10i), consisting of all and only the strings *ab, aabb, aaabbb,* ... can be produced by the [Σ, F] grammar (18).

(18)   Σ: *Z*

     F: *Z → ab*

         Z → aZb

---

[4]   See my "Three models for the description of language" (above, p. 22, fn. 3) for proofs of this and related theorems about relative power of grammars.

This grammar has the initial string Z (as (13) has the initial string *Sentence*) and it has two rules. It can easily be seen that each terminated derivation constructed from (18) ends in a string of the language (10i), and that all such strings are produced in this way. Similarly, languages of the form (10ii) can be produced by $[\Sigma, \text{F}]$ grammars (10iii), however, cannot be produced by a grammar of this type, unless the rules embody contextual restrictions.[5]

In § 3 we pointed out that the languages (10i) and (10ii) correspond to subparts of English, and that therefore the finite state Markov process model is not adequate for English. We now see that the phrase structure model does not fail in such cases. We have not proved the adequacy of the phrase structure model, but we have shown that large parts of English which literally cannot be described in terms of the finite-state process model can be described in terms of phrase structure.

Note that in the case of (18), we can say that in the string *aaabbb* of (10i), for example, *ab* is a Z, *aabb* is a Z, and *aaabbb* itself is a Z.[6] Thus this particular string contains three 'phrases,' each of which is a Z. This is, of course, a very trivial language. It is important to observe that in describing this language we have introduced a symbol Z which is not contained in the sentences of this language. This is the essential fact about phrase structure which gives it its 'abstract' character.

Observe also that in the case of both (13) and (18) (as in every system of phrase structure), each terminal string has many different representations. For example, in the case of (13), the terminal string "the man hit the ball" is represented by the strings *Sentence*, $NP + VP$, $T + N + VP$, and all the other lines of (14), as well as by such strings as $NP + Verb + NP$, $T + N + hit + NP$, which would occur in other derivations equivalent to (14) in the sense there defined. On the level of phrase structure, then, each sentence of the language is represented by a *set* of strings, not by a single string as it

---

[5] See my "On certain formal properties of grammars", *Information and Control* 2.133–167 (1959).

[6] Where "is a" is the relation defined in § 4.1 in terms of such diagrams as (15).

is on the level of phonemes, morphemes, or words. Thus phrase structure, taken as a linguistic level, has the fundamentally different and nontrivial character which, as we saw in the last paragraph of § 3, is required for some linguistic level. We cannot set up a hierarchy among the various representations of "the man hit the ball"; we cannot subdivide the system of phrase structure into a finite set of levels, ordered from higher to lower, with one representation for each sentence on each of these sublevels. For example, there is no way of ordering the elements *NP* and *VP* relative to one another. Noun phrases are contained within verb phrases, and verb phrases within noun phrases, in English. Phrase structure must be considered as a single level, with a set of representations for each sentence of the language. There is a one-one correspondence between the properly chosen sets of representations, and diagrams of the form (15).

4.3   Suppose that by a $[\Sigma, F]$ grammar we can generate all of the grammatical sequences of morphemes of a language. In order to complete the grammar we must state the phonemic structure of these morphemes, so that the grammar will produce the grammatical phoneme sequences of the language. But this statement (which we would call the *morphophonemics* of the language) can also be given by a set of rules of the form "rewrite X as Y", e.g., for English,

(19) (i)   *walk* → /wɔk/
    (ii)   *take + past* → /tuk/
    (iii)   *hit + past* → /hit/
    (iv)   /...D/ + *past* → /...D/ + /ɪd/ (where D = /t/ or /d/)
    (v)   /...C_{unv}/ + *past* → /...C_{unv}/ + /t/ (where C_{unv} is an unvoiced consonant)
    (vi)   *past* → /d/.
    (vii)   *take* → /teyk/
    etc.

or something similar. Note, incidentally, that order must be defined among these rules — e.g., (ii) must precede (v) or (vii), or we will derive such forms as /teykt/ for the past tense of *take*. In these morphophonemic rules we need no longer require that only a single symbol be rewritten in each rule.

We can now extend the phrase structure derivations by applying (19), so that we have a unified process for generating phoneme sequence from the initial string *Sentence*. This makes it appear as though the break between the higher level of phrase structure and the lower levels is arbitrary. Actually, the distinction is not arbitrary. For one thing, as we have seen, the formal properties of the rules $X \rightarrow Y$ corresponding to phrase structure are different from those of the morphophonemic rules, since in the case of the former we must require that only a single symbol be rewritten. Second, the elements that figure in the rules (19) can be classified into a finite set of levels (e.g., phonemes and morphemes; or, perhaps, phonemes, morphophonemes, and morphemes) each of which is elementary in the sense that a single string of elements of this level is associated with each sentence as its representation on this level (except in cases of homonymity), and each such string represents a single sentence. But the elements that appear in the rules corresponding to phrase structure cannot be classified into higher and lower levels in this way. We shall see below that there is an even more fundamental reason for marking this subdivison into the higher level rules of phrase structure and the lower level rules that convert strings of morphemes into strings of phonemes.

The formal properties of the system of phrase structure make an interesting study, and it is easy to show that further elaboration of the form of grammar is both necessary and possible. Thus it can easily be seen that it would be quite advantageous to order the rules of the set F so that certain of the rules can apply only after others have applied. For example, we should certainly want all rules of the form (17) to apply before any rule which enables us to rewrite *NP* as *NP + Preposition + NP*, or the like; otherwise the grammar will produce such nonsentences as "the men near the truck begins work at eight." But this elaboration leads to problems that would carry us beyond the scope of this study.

5

LIMITATIONS OF
PHRASE STRUCTURE DESCRIPTION

5.1 We have discussed two models for the structure of language, a communication theoretic model based on a conception of language as a Markov process and corresponding, in a sense, to the minimal linguistic theory, and a phrase structure model based on immediate constituent analysis. We have seen that the first is surely inadequate for the purposes of grammar, and that the second is more powerful than the first, and does not fail in the same way. Of course there are languages (in our general sense) that cannot be described in terms of phrase structure, but I do not know whether or not English is itself literally outside the range of such analysis. However, I think that there are other grounds for rejecting the theory of phrase structure as inadequate for the purpose of linguistic description.

The strongest possible proof of the inadequacy of a linguistic theory is to show that it literally cannot apply to some natural language. A weaker, but perfectly sufficient demonstration of inadequacy would be to show that the theory can apply only clumsily; that is, to show that any grammar that can be constructed in terms of this theory will be extremely complex, *ad hoc*, and 'unrevealing', that certain very simple ways of describing grammatical sentences cannot be accommodated within the associated forms of grammar, and that certain fundamental formal properties of natural language cannot be utilized to simplify grammars. We can gather a good deal of evidence of this sort in favor of the thesis that the form of grammar described above, and the conception of linguistic theory that underlies it, are fundamentally inadequate.

The only way to test the adequacy of our present apparatus is to attempt to apply it directly to the description of English sentences.

As soon as we consider any sentences beyond the simplest type, and in particular, when we attempt to define some order among the rules that produce these sentences, we find that we run into numerous difficulties and complications. To give substance to this claim would require a large expenditure of effort and space, and I can only assert here that this can be shown fairly convincingly.[1] Instead of undertaking this rather arduous and ambitious course here, I shall limit myself to sketching a few simple cases in which considerable improvement is possible over grammars of the form [Σ, F]. In § 8 I shall suggest an independent method of demonstrating the inadequacy of constituent analysis as a means of describing English sentence structure.

5.2   One of the most productive processes for forming new sentences is the process of conjunction. If we have two sentences $Z + X + W$ and $Z + Y + W$, and if X and Y are actually constituents of these sentences, we can generally form a new sentence $Z - X + and + Y - W$. For example, from the sentences (20a-b) we can form the new sentence (21).

(20)   (a) the scene – of the movie – was in Chicago

(b) the scene – of the play – was in Chicago

(21)   the scene – of the movie and of the play – was in Chicago.

If X and Y are, however, not constituents, we generally cannot do this.[2] For example we cannot form (23) from (22a-b).

---

[1]   See my *The logical structure of linguistic theory* for detailed analysis of this problem.

[2]   (21) and (23) are extreme cases in which there is no question about the possibility of conjunction. There are many less clear cases. For example, it is obvious that "John enjoyed the book and liked the play" (a string of the form $NP - VP + and + VP$) is a perfectly good sentence, but many would question the grammaticalness of, e.g., "John enjoyed and my friend liked the play" (a string of the form $NP + Verb + and + Verb - NP$). The latter sentence, in which conjunction crosses over constituent boundaries, is much less natural than the alternative "John enjoyed the play and my friend liked it", but there is no preferable alternative to the former. Such sentences with conjunction crossing constituent boundaries are also, in general, marked by special phonemic features such as extra long pauses (in our example, between "liked" and "the"), contrastive stress and intonation, failure to reduce vowels and drop final consonants in

(22) (a) the – liner sailed down the – river
      (b) the – tugboat chugged up the – river
(23) the – liner sailed down the and tugboat chugged up the – river.

Similarly, if X and Y are both constituents, but are constituents of different kinds (i.e., if in the diagram of the form (15) they each have a single origin, but this origin is labelled differently), then we cannot in general form a new sentence by conjunction. For example, we cannot form (25) from (24a-b).

(24) (a) the scene – of the movie – was in Chicago
      (b) the scene – that I wrote – was in Chicago
(25) the scene – of the movie and that I wrote – was in Chicago

In fact, the possibility of conjunction offers one of the best criteria for the initial determination of phrase structure. We can simplify the description of conjunction if we try to set up constituents in such a way that the following rule will hold:

(26) If S_1 and S_2 are grammatical sentences, and S_1 differs from S_2 only in that X appears in S_1 where Y appears in S_2 (i.e., $S_1 = ..X..$ and $S_2 = ..Y..$), and X and Y are constituents of the same type in S_1 and S_2, respectively, then S_3 is a sentence, where S_3 is the result of replacing X by $X + and + Y$ in S_1 (i.e., $S_3 = ..X + and + Y..$).

---

rapid speech, etc. Such features normally mark the reading of non-grammatical strings. The most reasonable way to describe this situation would seem to be by a description of the following kind: to form fully grammatical sentences by conjunction, it is necessary to conjoin single constituents; if we conjoin pairs of constituents, and these are major constituents (i.e., 'high up' in the diagram (15)), the resulting sentences are semi-grammatical; the more completely we violate constituent structure by conjunction, the less grammatical is the resulting sentence. This description requires that we generalize the grammatical-ungrammatical dichotomy, developing a notion of degree of grammaticalness. It is immaterial to our discussion, however, whether we decide to exclude such sentences as "John enjoyed and my friend liked the play" as ungrammatical, whether we include them as semi-grammatical, or whether we include them as fully grammatical but with special phonemic features. In any event they form a class of utterances distinct from "John enjoyed the play and liked the book," etc., where constituent structure is preserved perfectly; and our conclusion that the rule for conjunction must make explicit reference to constituent structure therefore stands, since this distinction will have to be pointed out in the grammar.

Even though additional qualification is necessary here, the grammar is enormously simplified if we set up constituents in such a way that (26) holds even approximately. That is, it is easier to state the distribution of "and" by means of qualifications on this rule than to do so directly without such a rule. But we now face the following difficulty: we cannot incorporate the rule (26) or anything like it ir a grammar $[\Sigma, F]$ of phrase structure, because of certain fundamental limitations on such grammars. The essential property of rule (26) is that in order to apply it to sentences S_1 and S_2 to form the new sentence S_3 we must know not only the actual form of S_1 and S_2 but also their constituent structure — we must know not only the final shape of these sentences, but also their 'history of derivation.' But each rule $X \rightarrow Y$ of the grammar $[\Sigma, F]$ applies or fails to apply to a given string by virtue of the actual substance of this string. The question of how this string gradually assumed this form is irrelevant. If the string contains X as a substring, the rule $X \rightarrow Y$ can apply to it; if not, the rule cannot apply.

We can put this somewhat differently. The grammar $[\Sigma, F]$ can also be regarded as a very elementary process that generates sentences not from "left to right" but from "top to bottom". Suppose that we have the following grammar of phrase structure:

(27) Σ: *Sentence*

    F: $X_1 \rightarrow Y_1$

          $\vdots$

        $X_n \rightarrow Y_n$.

Then we can represent this grammar as a machine with a finite number of internal states, including an initial and a final state. In its initial state it can produce only the element *Sentence*, thereby moving into a new state. It can then produce any string Y_i such that *Sentence* $\rightarrow Y_i$ is one of the rules of F in (27), again moving into a new state. Suppose that Y_i is the string ... X_j ... Then the machine can produce the string ... Y_j ... by "applying" the rule $X_j \rightarrow Y_j$. The machine proceeds in this way from state to state until it finally produces a terminal string; it is now in the final state. The machine thus produces derivations, in the sense of §4. The important point is that the state of the machine is completely determined by the string it has just produced (i.e., by the last step of the derivation); more specifically, the state is determined by the subset of 'left-hand' elements X_i of F which are contained in this last-produced string. But rule (26) requires a more powerful machine, which can "look back" to earlier strings in the derivation in order to determine how to produce the next step in the derivation.

Rule (26) is also fundamentally new in a different sense. It makes essential reference to two distinct sentences S_1 and S_2, but in grammars of the [Σ, F] type, there is no way to incorporate such double reference. The fact that rule (26) cannot be incorporated into the grammar of phrase structure indicates that even if this form for grammar is not literally inapplicable to English, it is certainly inadequate in the weaker but sufficient sense considered above. This rule leads to a considerable simplification of the grammar; in fact, it provides one of the best criteria for determining how to set up constituents. We shall see that there are many other rules of the same general type as (26) which play the same dual role.

5.3 In the grammar (13) we gave only one way of analyzing the element *Verb*, namely, as *hit* (cf. (13 vi)). But even with the verbal root fixed (let us say, as *take*), there are many other forms that this element can assume, e.g., *takes, has + taken, will + take, has + been + taken, is + being + taken,* etc. The study of these "auxiliary verbs" turns out to be quite crucial in the development of English grammar. We shall see that their behavior is very regular and simply describable when observed from a point of view that is quite different from that developed above. though it appears to be quite complex if we attempt to incorporate these phrases directly into a [Σ, F] grammar.

Consider first the auxiliaries that appear unstressed; for example, "has" in "John has read the book" but not "does" in "John *does* read books."[3] We can state the occurrence of these auxiliaries in declarative sentences by adding to the grammar (13) the following rules:

---

[3] We return to the stressed auxiliary "do" below, in § 7.1 (45)–(47).

(28) (i) $Verb \rightarrow Aux + V$

   (ii) $V \rightarrow hit, take, walk, read$, etc.

  (iii) $Aux \rightarrow C(M) (have + en) (be + ing) (be + en)$

   (iv) $M \rightarrow will, can, may, shall, must$

(29) (i) $C \rightarrow \begin{cases} S \text{ in the context } NP_{sing}- \\ \varnothing \text{ in the context } NP_{pl}- \\ past \end{cases}$ [4]

   (ii) Let Af stand for any of the affixes $past, S, \varnothing, en, ing$. Let v stand for any M or V, or $have$ or be (i.e., for any non-affix in the phrase $Verb$). Then:

   $$Af + v \rightarrow v + Af \#,$$

   where $\#$ is interpreted as word boundary.[5]

  (iii) Replace $+$ by $\#$ except in the context $v - Af$. Insert $\#$ initially and finally.

The interpretation of the notations in (28 iii) is as follows: we must choose the element C, and we may choose zero or more of the parenthesized elements in the given order. In (29 i) we may develop C into any of three morphemes, observing the contextual restrictions given. As an example of the application of these rules, we construct a derivation in the style of (14), omitting the initial steps.

(30) $the + man + Verb + the + book$ from (13 i-v)

      $the + man + Aux + V + the + book$ (28 i)

      $the + man + Aux + read + the + book$ (28 ii)

      $the + man + C + have + en + be + ing + read + the + book$

                             (28 iii) – we select the elements C, $have + en$ and $be + ing$.

    $the + man + S + have + en + be + ing + read + the + book$

                             (29 i)

---

[4] We assume here that (13 ii) has been extended in the manner of fn. 3, above, p. 29, or something similar.

[5] If we were formulating the theory of grammar more carefully, we would interpret $\#$ as the concatenation operator on the level of words, while $+$ is the concatention operator on the level of phrase structure. (29) would then be part of the definition of a mapping which carries certain objects on the level of phrase structure (essentially, diagrams of the form (15)) into strings of words. See my *The logical structure of linguistic theory* for a more careful formulation.

the + *man* + *have* + *S* # *be* + *en* # *read* + *ing* # *the* + *book*
                                                        (29 ii) – three times.
the # *man* # *have* + *S* # *be* + *en* # *read* + *ing* # *the* # *book*
                                                        (29 iii)

The morphophonemic rules (19), etc., will convert the last line of
this derivation into:

(31)   the man has been reading the book

in phonemic transcription. Similarly, every other auxiliary verb
phrase can be generated. We return later to the question of further
restrictions that must be placed on these rules so that only grammatical sequences can be generated. Note, incidentally, that the
morphophonemic rules will have to include such rules as: *will* + *S* →
will, *will* + *past* → *would*. These rules can be dropped if we rewrite
(28 iii) so that either *C* or *M*, but not both, can be selected. But now
the forms *would*, *could*, *might*, *should* must be added to (28 iv), and
certain 'sequence of tense' statements become more complex. It is
immateral to our further discussion which of these alternative
analysesis iadopted. Several other minor revisions are possible.

Notice that in order to apply (29 i) in (30) we had to use the fact
that *the* + *man* is a singular noun phrase NP_{sing}. That is, we had to
refer back to some earlier step in the derivation in order to determine
the constituent structure of *the* + *man*. (The alternative of ordering
(29 i) and the rule that develops NP_{sing} into *the* + *man* in such a way
that (29 i) must precede the latter is not possible, for a variety of
reasons, some of which appear below). Hence, (29 i), just like (26),
goes beyond the elementary Markovian character of grammars of
phrase structure, and cannot be incorporated within the [Σ. F]
grammar.

Rule (29 ii) violates the requirements of [Σ, F] grammars even
more severely. It also requires reference to constituent structure
(i.e., past history of derivation) and in addition, we have no way to
express the required inversion within the terms of phrase structure.
Note that this rule is useful elsewhere in the grammar, at least in
the case where *Af* is *ing*. Thus the morphemes *to* and *ing* play a very

similar role within the noun phrase in that they convert verb phrases into noun phrases, giving, e.g.,

(32) $\left\{ \begin{array}{l} \text{to prove that theorem} \\ \text{proving that theorem} \end{array} \right\}$ was difficult.

etc. We can exploit this parallel by adding to the grammar (13) the rule

(33) $NP \rightarrow \left\{ \begin{array}{l} ing \\ to \end{array} \right\} VP$

The rule (29 ii) will then convert $ing + prove + that + theorem$ into $proving \# that + theorem$. A more detailed analysis of the VP shows that this parallel extends much further than this, in fact.

The reader can easily determine that to duplicate the effect of (28 iii) and (29) without going beyond the bounds of a system $[\Sigma, F]$ of phrase structure, it would be necessary to give a fairly complex statement. Once again, as in the case of conjunction, we see that significant simplification of the grammar is possible if we are permitted to formulate rules of a more complex type than those that correspond to a system of immediate constituent analysis. By allowing ourselves the freedom of (29 ii) we have been able to state the constituency of the auxiliary phrase in (28 iii) without regard to the interdependence of its elements, and it is always easier to describe a sequence of independent elements than a sequence of mutually dependent ones. To put the same thing differently, in the auxiliary verb phrase we really have discontinuous elements – e.g., in (30), the elements *have..en* and *be..ing*. But discontinuities cannot be handled within $[\Sigma, F]$ grammars.[6] In (28 iii) we treated these

---

[6] We might attempt to extend the notions of phrase structure to account for discontinuities. It has been pointed out several times that fairly serious difficulties arise in any systematic attempt to pursue this course. Cf. my "System of syntactic analysis," *Journal of Symbolic Logic* 18.242–56 (1953); C. F. Hockett, "A formal statement of morphemic analysis," *Studies in Linguistics* 10.27–39 (1952); idem, "Two models of grammatical description," *Linguistics Today, Word* 10.210–33 (1954). Similarly, one might seek to remedy some of the other deficiencies of $[\Sigma, F]$ grammars by a more complex account of phrase structure. I think that such an approach is ill-advised, and that it can only lead to the development of *ad hoc* and fruitless elaborations. It appears to be the case that the notions of phrase structure are quite adequate for a small

elements as continuous, and we introduced the discontinuity by the very simple additional rule (29 ii). We shall see below, in § 7, that this analysis of the element *Verb* serves as the basis for a far-reaching and extremely simple analysis of several important features of English syntax.

5.4 As a third example of the inadequacy of the conceptions of phrase structure, consider the case of the active-passive relation. Passive sentences are formed by selecting the element *be* + *en* in rule (28 iii). But there are heavy restrictions on this element that make it unique among the elements of the auxiliary phrase. For one thing, *be* + *en* can be selected only if the following *V* is transitive (e.g., *was* + *eaten* is permitted, but not *was* + *occurred*); but with a few exceptions the other elements of the auxiliary phrase can occur freely with verbs. Furthermore, *be* + *en* cannot be selected if the verb *V* is followed by a noun phrase, as in (30) (e.g., we cannot in general have *NP* + *is* + *V* + *en* + *NP*, even when *V* is transitive — we cannot have "lunch is eaten John"). Furthermore, if *V* is transitive and is followed by the prepositional phrase *by* + *NP*, then we *must* select *be* + *en* (we can have "lunch is eaten by John" but not "John is eating by lunch," etc.). Finally, note that in elaborating (13) into a full-fledged grammar we will have to place many restrictions on the choice of *V* in terms of subject and object in order to permit such sentences as: "John admires sincerity," "sincerity frightens John," "John plays golf," "John drinks wine," while excluding the 'inverse' non-sentences[7] "sincerity admires John," "John frightens sincerity,"

---

part of the language and that the rest of the language can be derived by repeated application of a rather simple set of transformations to the strings given by the phrase structure grammar. If we were to attempt to extend phrase structure grammar to cover the entire language directly, we would lose the simplicity of the limited phrase structure grammar and of the transformational development. This approach would miss the main point of level construction (cf. first paragraph of § 3.1), namely, to rebuild the vast complexity of the actual language more elegantly and systematically by extracting the contribution to this complexity of several linguistic levels, each of which is simple in itself.

[7] Here too we might make use of a notion of levels of grammaticalness as suggested in footnote 2, p. 35. Thus "sincerity admires John," though clearly less grammatical than "John admires sincerity," is certainly more grammatical

"golf plays John," "wine drinks John". But this whole network of restrictions fails completely when we choose $be + en$ as part of the auxiliary verb. In fact, in this case the same selectional dependencies hold, but in the opposite order. That is, for every sentence $NP_1 - V - NP_2$ we can have a corresponding sentence $NP_2 - is + Ven - by + NP_1$. If we try to include passives directly in the grammar (13), we shall have to restate all of these restrictions in the opposite order for the case in which $be + en$ is chosen as part of the auxiliary verb. This inelegant duplication, as well as the special restrictions involving the element $be + en$, can be avoided only if we deliberately exclude passives from the grammar of phrase structure, and reintroduce them by a rule such as:

(34)   If S_1 is a grammatical sentence of the form
$$NP_1 - Aux - V - NP_2,$$
then the corresponding string of the form
$$NP_2 - Aux + be + en - V - by + NP_1$$
is also a grammatical sentence.

For example, if $John - C - admire - sincerity$ is a sentence, then $sincerity - C + be + en - admire - by + John$ (which by (29) and (19) becomes "sincerity is admired by John") is also a sentence.

We can now drop the element $be + en$, and all of the special restrictions associated with it, from (28 iii). The fact that $be + en$ requires a transitive verb, that it cannot occur before $V + NP$, that it must occur before $V + by + NP$ (where V is transitive), that it inverts the order of the surrounding noun phrases, is in each case an automatic consequence of rule (34). This rule thus leads to a considerable simplification of the grammar. But (34) is well beyond the limits of $[\Sigma, F]$ grammars. Like (29 ii), it requires reference to the constituent structure of the string to which it applies and it carries out an inversion on this string in a structurally determined manner.

---

than "of admires John," I believe that a workable notion of degree of grammaticalness can be developed in purely formal terms (cf. my *The logical structure of linguistic theory*), but this goes beyond the bounds of the present discussion. See § 7.5 for an even stronger demonstration that inversion is necessary in the passive.

5.5 We have discussed three rules ((26), (29), (34)) which materially simplify the description of English but which cannot be incorporated into a [Σ, F] grammar. There are a great many other rules of this type, a few of which we shall discuss below. By further study of the limitations of phrase structure grammars with respect to English we can show quite conclusively that these grammars will be so hope-lessly complex that they will be without interest unless we incorporate such rules.

If we examine carefully the implications of these supplementary rules, however, we see that they lead to an entirely new conception of linguistic structure. Let us call each such rule a "grammatical transformation." A grammatical transformation T operates on a given string (or, as in the case of (26), on a set of strings) with a given constituent structure and converts it into a new string with a new derived constituent structure. To show exactly *how* this operation is performed requires a rather elaborate study which would go far beyond the scope of these remarks, but we can in fact develop a certain fairly complex but reasonably natural algebra of transformations having the properties that we apparently require for grammatical description.[8]

From these few examples we can already detect some of the essential properties of a transformational grammar. For one thing, it is clear that we must define an order of application on these transformations. The passive transformation (34), for example, must apply *before* (29). It must precede (29i), in particular, so that the verbal element in the resulting sentence will have the same number as the new grammatical subject of the passive sentence. And it must precede (29ii) so that the latter rule will apply properly to the new inserted element *be + en*. (In discussing the question of whether or not (29i) can be fitted into a [Σ, F] grammar, we mentioned that this rule could not be required to apply before the rule

---

    [8]   See my "Three models for the description of language" (above, p. 22, fn. 3)
for a brief account of transformations, and *The logical structure of linguistic theory* and *Transformational Analysis* for a detailed development of trans-formational algebra and transformational grammars. See Z. S. Harris, "Cooc-currence and Transformations in linguistic structure," *Language* 33.283–340 (1957), for a somewhat different approach to transformational analysis.

analyzing NP_{sing} into *the + man*, etc. One reason for this is now obvious — (29i) must apply after (34), but (34) must apply after the analysis of NP_{sing}, or we will not have the proper selectional relations between the subject and verb and the verb and 'agent' in the passive.)

Secondly, note that certain transformations are *obligatory*, whereas others are only *optional*. For example, (29) must be applied to every derivation, or the result will simply not be a sentence.[9] But (34), the passive transformation, may or may not be applied in any particular case. Either way the result is a sentence. Hence (29) is an obligatory transformation and (34) is an optional transformation.

This distinction between obligatory and optional transformations leads us to set up a fundamental distinction among the sentences of the language. Suppose that we have a grammar G with a [Σ, F] part and a transformational part, and suppose that the transformational part has certain obligatory transformations and certain optional ones. Then we define the *kernel* of the language (in terms of the grammar G) as the set of sentences that are produced when we apply obligatory transformations to the terminal strings of the [Σ, F] grammar. The transformational part of the grammar will be set up in such a way that transformations can apply to kernel sentences (more correctly, to the forms that underlie kernel sentences — i.e., to terminal strings of the [Σ, F] part of the grammar) or to prior transforms. Thus every sentence of the language will either belong to the kernel or will be derived from the strings underlying one or more kernel sentences by a sequence of one or more transformations.

From these considerations we are led to a picture of grammars as possessing a natural tripartite arrangement. Corresponding to the level of phrase structure, a grammar has a sequence of rules of the form $X \rightarrow Y$, and corresponding to lower levels it has a sequence of

---

[9] But of the three parts of (29i), only the third is obligatory. That is, *past* may occur after NP_{sing}- or NP_{pl}. Whenever we have an element such as C in (29i) which must be developed, but perhaps in several alternative ways, we can order the alternatives and make each one but the last optional, and the last, obligatory.

morphophonemic rules of the same basic form. Linking these two sequences, it has a sequence of transformational rules. Thus the grammar will look something like this:

(35) Σ: *Sentence*:

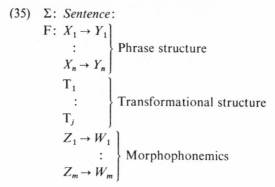

$$
\left. \begin{array}{l} \text{F: } X_1 \to Y_1 \\ \qquad : \\ X_n \to Y_n \end{array} \right\} \text{Phrase structure}
$$

$$
\left. \begin{array}{l} T_1 \\ \ : \\ T_j \end{array} \right\} \text{Transformational structure}
$$

$$
\left. \begin{array}{l} Z_1 \to W_1 \\ \qquad : \\ Z_m \to W_m \end{array} \right\} \text{Morphophonemics}
$$

To produce a sentence from such a grammar we construct an extended derivation beginning with *Sentence*. Running through the rules of F we construct a terminal string that will be a sequence of morphemes, though not necessarily in the correct order. We then run through the sequence of transformations T_1, ... T_j, applying each obligatory one and perhaps certain optional ones. These transformations may rearrange strings or may add or delete morphemes. As a result they yield a string of words. We then run through the morphophonemic rules, thereby converting this string of words into a string of phonemes. The phrase structure segment of the grammar will include such rules as those of (13), (17) and (28). The transformational part will include such rules as (26), (29) and (34), formulated properly in the terms that must be developed in a full-scale theory of transformations. The morphophonemic part will include such rules as (19). This sketch of the process of generation of sentences must (and easily can) be generalized to allow for proper functioning of such rules as (26) which operate on a set of sentences, and to allow transformations to reapply to transforms so that more and more complex sentences can be produced.

When we apply only obligatory transformations in the generation of a given sentence, we call the resulting sentence a kernel sentence. Further investigation would show that in the phrase structure and morphophonemic parts of the grammar we can also extract a skeleton of obligatory rules that *must* be applied whenever we reach them in the process of generating a sentence. In the last few paragraphs of § 4 we pointed out that the phrase structure rules lead to a conception of linguistic structure and "level of representation" that is fundamentally different from that provided by the morphophonemic rules. On each of the lower levels corresponding to the lower third of the grammar an utterance is, in general, represented by a single sequence of elements. But phrase structure cannot be broken down into sublevels: on the level of phrase structure an utterance is represented by a set of strings that cannot be ordered into higher or lower levels. This set of representing strings is equivalent to a diagram of the form (15). On the transformational level, an utterance is represented even more abstractly in terms of a sequence of transformations by which it is derived, ultimately from kernel sentences (more correctly, from the strings which underlie kernel sentences). There is a very natural general definition of "linguistic level" that includes all of these cases,[10] and as we shall see later, there is good reason to consider each of these structures to be a linguistic level.

When transformational analysis is properly formulated we find that it is essentially more powerful than description in terms of phrase structure, just as the latter is essentially more powerfull than description in terms of finite state Markov processes that generate sentences from left to right. In particular, such languages as (10iii) which lie beyond the bounds of phrase structure description with context-free rules can be derived transformationally.[11] It is important to observe that the grammar is materially simplified when we add a transformational level, since it is now necessary to provide phrase structure directly only for kernel sentences — the terminal strings of the [Σ, F] grammar are just those which underlie kernel

---

[10]   Cf. *The logical structure of linguistic theory* and *Transformational Analysis*.

[11]   Let G be a [Σ, F] grammar with the initial string *Sentence* and with the set of all finite strings of a's and b's as its terminal output. There is such a grammar. Let G' be the grammar which contains G as its phrase structure part, supplemented by the transformation T that operates on any string K which is a *Sentence*, converting it into $K + K$. Then the output of G' is (10iii). Cf. p. 31.

sentences. We choose the kernel sentences in such a way that the terminal strings underlying the kernel are easily derived by means of a [Σ, F] description, while all other sentences can be derived from these terminal strings by simply statable transformations. We have seen, and shall see again below, several examples of simplifications resulting from transformational analysis. Full-scale syntactic investigation of English provides a great many more cases.

One further point about grammars of the form (35) deserves mention, since it has apparently led to some misunderstanding. We have described these grammars as devices for generating sentences. This formulation has occasionally led to the idea that there is a certain asymmetry in grammatical theory in the sense that grammar is taking the point of view of the speaker rather than the hearer; that it is concerned with the process of producing utterances rather than the 'inverse' process of analyzing and reconstructing the structure of given utterances. Actually, grammars of the form that we have been discussing are quite neutral as between speaker and hearer, between synthesis and analysis of utterances. A grammar does not tell us how to synthesize a specific utterance; it does not tell us how to analyze a particular given utterance. In fact, these two tasks which the speaker and hearer must perform are essentially the same, and are both outside the scope of grammars of the form (35). Each such grammar is simply a description of a certain set of utterances, namely, those which it generates. From this grammar we can reconstruct the formal relations that hold among these utterances in terms of the notions of phrase structure, transformational structure, etc. Perhaps the issue can be clarified by an analogy to a part of chemical theory concerned with the structurally possible compounds. This theory might be said to generate all physically possible compounds just as a grammar generates all grammatically 'possible' utterances. It would serve as a theoretical basis for techniques of qualitative analysis and synthesis of specific compounds, just as one might rely on a grammar in the investigation of such special problems as analysis and synthesis of particular utterances.

6

ON THE GOALS OF LINGUISTIC THEORY

6.1 In §§ 3, 4 two models of linguistic structure were developed: a simple communication theoretic model and a formalized version of immediate constituent analysis. Each was found to be inadequate, and in § 5 I suggested a more powerful model combining phrase structure and grammatical transformations that might remedy these inadequacies. Before going on to explore this possiblity, I would like to clarify certain points of view that underlie the whole approach of his study.

Our fundamental concern throughout this discussion of linguistic structure is the problem of justification of grammars. A grammar of the language L is essentially a theory of L. Any scientific theory is based on a finite number of observations, and it seeks to relate the observed phenomena and to predict new phenomena by constructing general laws in terms of hypothetical constructs such as (in physics, for example) "mass" and "electron." Similarly, a grammar of English is based on a finite corpus of utterances (observations), and it will contain certain grammatical rules (laws) stated in terms of the particular phonemes, phrases, etc., of English (hypothetical constructs). These rules express structural relations among the sentences of the corpus and the indefinite number of sentences generated by the grammar beyond the corpus (predictions). Our problem is to develop and clarify the criteria for selecting the correct grammar for each language, that is, the correct theory of this language.

Two types of criteria were mentioned in § 2.1. Clearly, every grammar will have to meet certain *external conditions of adequacy*; e.g., the sentences generated will have to be acceptable to the native speaker. In § 8 we shall consider several other external conditions of this sort. In addition, we pose a *condition of generality* on grammars; we require that the grammar of a given language be constructed in accordance with a specific theory of linguistic structure in which such terms as "phoneme" and "phrase" are defined independently of any particular language.[1] If we drop either the external conditions or the generality requirement, there will be no way to choose among a vast number of totally different 'grammars,' each compatible with a given corpus. But, as we observed in § 2.1, these requirements jointly give us a very strong test of adequacy for a general theory of linguistic structure and the set of grammars that it provides for particular languages.

Notice that neither the general theory nor the particular grammars are fixed for all time, in this view. Progress and revision may come from the discovery of new facts about particular languages, or from purely theoretical insights about organization of linguistic data — that is, new models for linguistic structure. But there is also no circularity in this conception. At any given time we can attempt to formulate as precisely as possible both the general theory and the set of associated grammars that must meet the empirical, external conditions of adequacy.

We have not yet considered the following very crucial question: What is the relation between the general theory and the particular grammars that follow from it? In other words, what sense can we give to the notion "follow from," in this context? It is at this point that our approach will diverge sharply from many theories of linguistic structure.

The strongest requirement that could be placed on the relation between a theory of linguistic structure and particular grammars is that the theory must provide a practical and mechanical method for

---

[1] I presume that these two conditions are similar to what Hjelmslev has in mind when he speaks of the *appropriateness* and *arbitrariness* of linguistic theory. Cf. L. Hjelmslev, *Prolegomena to a theory of language = Memoir 7, Indiana University Publications Antropology and Linguistics* (Baltimore, 1953), p. 8. See also Hockett's discussion of "metacriteria" for linguistics ("Two models of grammatical description," *Linguistics Today, Word* 10.232-3) in this connection.

actually constructing the grammar, given a corpus of utterances. Let us say that such a theory provides us with a *discovery procedure* for grammars.

A weaker requirement would be that the theory must provide a practical and mechanical method for determining whether or not a grammar proposed for a given corpus is, in fact, the best grammar of the language from which this corpus is drawn. Such a theory, which is not concerned with the question of *how* this grammar was constructed, might be said to provide a *decision procedure* for grammars.

An even weaker requirement would be that given a corpus and given two proposed grammars G_1 and G_2, the theory must tell us which is the better grammar of the language from which the corpus is drawn. In this case we might say that the theory provides an *evaluation procedure* for grammars.

These theories can be represented graphically in the following manner.

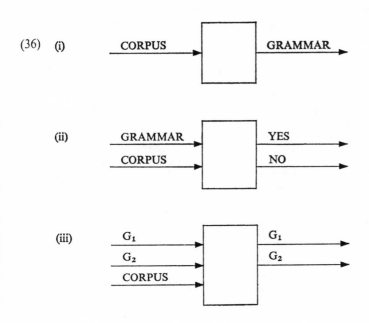

Figure (36i) represents a theory conceived as a machine with a corpus as its input and a grammar as its output; hence, a theory that provides a discovery procedure. (36ii) is a device with a grammar and a corpus as its inputs, and the answers "yes" or "no" as its outputs, as the grammar is or is not the correct one; hence, it represents a theory that provides a decision procedure for grammars. (36iii) represents a theory with grammars G_1 and G_2 and a corpus as inputs, and the more preferable of G_1 and G_2 as output; hence a theory that provides an evaluation procedure for grammars.[2]

The point of view adopted here is that it is unreasonable to demand of linguistic theory that it provide anything more than a practical evaluation procedure for grammars. That is, we adopt the weakest of the three positions described above. As I interpret most of the more careful proposals for the development of linguistic theory,[3] they attempt to meet the strongest of these three requirements. That is, they attempt to state methods of analysis that an investigator might actually use, if he had the time, to construct a grammar of a language directly from the raw data. I think that it is very questionable that this goal is attainable in any interesting way,

---

[2] The basic question at issue is not changed if we are willing to accept a small set of correct grammars instead of a single one.

[3] For example, B. Bloch, "A set of postulates for phonemic analysis," *Language* 24.3–46 (1948); N. Chomsky, "Systems of syntactic analysis," *Journal of Symbolic Logic* 18.242–56 (1953); Z. S. Harris, "From phoneme to morpheme," *Language* 31.190–222 (1955); idem, *Methods in structural linguistics* (Chicago, 1951); C. F. Hockett, "A formal statement of morphemic analysis," *Studies in Linguistics* 10.27–39 (1952); idem, "Problems of morphemic analysis," *Language* 23.321–43 (1947); R. S. Wells, "Immediate constituents," *Language* 23.81–117 (1947); and many other works. Although discovery procedures are the explicit goal of these works, we often find on careful examination that the theory that has actually been constructed furnishes no more than an evaluation procedure for grammars. For example, Hockett states his aim in "A formal statement of morphemic analysis" as the development of "formal procedures by which one can work from scratch to a complete description of the pattern of a language" (p. 27); but what he actually does is describe some of the formal properties of a morphological analysis and then propose a "criterion whereby the relative efficiency of two possible morphic solutions can be determined; with that, we can choose the maximally efficient possibility, or, arbitrarily, any one of those which are equally efficient but more efficient than all others" (p. 29).

and I suspect that any attempt to meet it will lead into a maze of more and more elaborate and complex analytic procedures that will fail to provide answers for many important questions about the nature of linguistic structure. I believe that by lowering our sights to the more modest goal of developing an evaluation procedure for grammars we can focus attention more clearly on really crucial problems of linguistic structure and we can arrive at more satisfying answers to them. The correctness of this judgment can only be determined by the actual development and comparison of theories of these various sorts. Notice, however, that the weakest of these three requirements is still strong enough to guarentee significance for a theory that meets it. There are few areas of science in which one would seriously consider the possibility of developing a general, practical, mechanical method for choosing among several theories, each compatible with the available data.

In the case of each of these conceptions of linguistic theory we have qualified the characterization of the type of procedure by the word "practical". This vague qualification is crucial for an empirical science. Suppose, for example, that we were to evaluate grammars by measuring some such simple property as length. Then it would be correct to say that we have a practical evaluation procedure for grammars, since we could count the number of symbols they contain; and it would also be literally correct to say that we have a discovery procedure, since we can order all sequences of the finite number of symbols from which grammars are constructed in terms of length, and we can test each of these sequences to see if it is a grammar, being sure that after some finite amount of time we shall find the shortest sequence that qualifies. But this is not the type of discovery procedure that is contemplated by those who are attempting to meet the strong requirement discussed above.

Suppose that we use the word "simplicity" to refer to the set of formal properties of grammars that we shall consider in choosing among them. Then there are three main tasks in the kind of program for linguistic theory that we have suggested. First, it is necessary to state precisely (if possible, with operational, behavioral tests) the external criteria of adequacy for grammars. Second, we

54   SYNTACTIC STRUCTURES

must characterize the form of grammars in a general and explicit way so that we can actually propose grammars of this form for particular languages. Third, we must analyze and define the notion of simplicity that we intend to use in choosing among grammars all of which are of the proper form. Completion of the latter two tasks will enable us to formulate a general theory of linguistic structure in which such notions as "phoneme in L", "phrase in L", "transformation in L" are defined for an arbitrary language L in terms of physical and distributional properties of utterances of L and formal properties of grammars of L.[4] For example, we shall define the set of phonemes of L as a set of elements which have certain physical and distributional properties, and which appear in the simplest grammar for L. Given such a theory, we can attempt to construct grammars for actual languages, and we can determine whether or not the simplest grammars that we can find (i.e., the grammars that the general theory compels us to choose) meet the external conditions of adequacy. We shall continue to revise our notions of simplicity and out characterization of the form of grammars until the grammars selected by the theory do meet the external conditions.[5] Notice that this theory may not tell us, in any practical way, how to actually go about constructing the grammar of a given language from a corpus. But it must tell us how to evaluate such a grammar; it must thus enable us to choose between two proposed grammars.

In the preceding sections of this study we have been concerned with the second of these three tasks. We have assumed that the set of grammatical sentences of English is given and that we have some notion of simplicity, and we have tried to determine what sort of grammar will generate exactly the grammatical sentences in some simple way. To formulate this goal in somewhat different terms,

---

[4] Linguistic theory will thus be formulated in a metalanguage to the language in which grammars are written — a metametalanguage to any language for which a grammar is constructed.

[5] We may in fact revise the criteria of adequacy, too, in the course of research. That is, we may decide that certain of these tests do not apply to grammatical phenomena. The subject matter of a theory is not completely determined in advance of investigation. It is partially determined by the possibility of giving an organized and systematic account of some range of phenomena.

we remarked above that one of the notions that must be defined in general linguistic theory is "sentence in L." Entering into the definitions will be such terms as "observed utterance in L", "simplicity of the grammar of L," etc. This general theory is accordingly concerned with clarifying the relation between the set of grammatical sentence and the set of observed sentences. Our investigation of the structure of the former set is a preparatory study, proceeding from the assumption that before we can characterize this relation clearly, we will have to know a great deal more about the formal properties of each of these sets.

In § 7 below, we shall continue to investigate the relative complexity of various ways of describing English structure. In particular, we shall be concerned with the question of whether the whole grammar is simplified if we consider a certain class of sentences to be kernel sentences or if we consider them to be derived by transformation. We thus arrive at certain decisions about the structure of English. In § 8 we shall argue that there is independent evidence in favor of our method for selecting grammars. That is, we shall try to show that the simpler grammars meet certain external conditions of adequacy while the more complex grammars that embody different decisions about assignment of sentences to the kernel, etc., fail these conditions. These results can be no more than suggestive, however, until we give a rigorous account of the notion of simplicity employed. I think that such an account can be given, but this would go beyond the scope of the present monograph. Nevertheless, it should be fairly clear that under any reasonable definition of "simplicity of grammar", most of the decisions about relative complexity that we reach below will stand.[6]

Notice that simplicity is a *systematic* measure; the only ultimate

---

[6]   See my *The logical structure of linguistic theory* for discussion of methods for evaluating grammars in terms of formal properties of simplicity.

We are not, incidentally, denying the usefullness of even partially adequate discovery procedures. They may provide valuable hints to the practicing linguist or they may lead to a small set of grammars that can then be evaluated. Our main point is that a linguistic theory should not be identified with a manual of useful procedures, nor should it be expected to provide mechanical procedures for the discovery of grammars.

criterion in evaluation is the simplicity of the whole system. In discussing particular cases, we can only indicate how one or another decision will affect the over-all complexity. Such validation can only be tentative, since by simplifying one part of the grammar we may complicate other parts. It is when we find that simplification of one part of the grammar leads to corresponding simplification of other parts that we feel that we are really on the right track. Below, we shall try to show that the simplest transformational analysis of one class of sentences does quite frequently clear the way to a simpler analysis of other classes.

In short, we shall never consider the question of how one might have arrived at the grammar whose simplicity is being determined; e.g., how one might have discovered the analysis of the verb phrase presented in § 5.3. Question of this sort are not relevant to the program of research that we have outlined above. One may arrive at a grammar by intuition, guess-work, all sorts of partial methodological hints, reliance on past experience, etc. It is no doubt possible to give an organized account of many useful procedures of analysis, but it is questionable whether these can be formulated rigorously, exhaustively and simply enough to qualify as a practical and mechanical discovery procedure. At any rate, this problem is not within the scope of our investigations here. Our ultimate aim is to provide an objective, non-intuitive way to evaluate a grammar once presented, and to compare it with other proposed grammars. We are thus interested in describing the form of grammars (equivalently, the nature of linguistic structure) and investigating the empirical consequences of adopting a certain model for linguistic structure, rather than in showing how, in principe, one might have arrived at the grammar of a language.

6.2 Once we have disclaimed any intention of finding a practical discovery procedure for grammars, certain problems that have been the subject of intense methodological controversy simply do not arise. Consider the problem of interdependence of levels. It has been correctly pointed out that if morphemes are defined in terms of phonemes, and, simultaneously, morphological considerations are considered relevant to phonemic analysis, then linguistic theory may be nullified by a real circularity. However, interdependence of levels does not necessarily lead to circularity. In this case, for example, we can define "tentative phoneme set" and "tentative morpheme set" independently and we can develop a relation of compatibility that holds between tentative phoneme sets and tentative morpheme sets. We can then define a pair of a phoneme set and a morpheme set for a given language as a compatible pair of a tentative phoneme set and a tentative morpheme set. Our compatibility relation may be framed partially in terms of simplicity considerations; that is, we may define the phonemes and morphemes of a language as the tentative phonemes and morphemes which, among other things, jointly lead to the simplest grammar. This gives us a perfectly straightforward way to define interdependent levels with no circularity. Of course, it does not tell us how to *find* the phonemes and morphemes in a direct, mechanical way. But no other phonemic or morphological theory really meets this strong requirement either, and there is little reason to believe that it can be met significantly. In any event, when we lower our aims to the development of an evaluation procedure, there remains little motivation for any objection to mixing of levels, and there is no difficulty in avoiding circularity in the definition of interdependent levels.[7]

---

[7] See Z. S. Harris, *Methods in structural linguistics* (Chicago, 1951) (e.g., *Appendix to 7.4, Appendix to 8.2*, chapters 9, 12) for examples of procedures which lead to interdependent levels. I think that Fowler's objections to Harris' morphological procedures (cf.. *Language* 28.504–9 [1952]) can be met without difficulty by a noncircular formulation of the type just proposed. Cf. C. F. Hockett, *A manual of phonology* = *Memoir 11, Indiana University Publications in Anthropology and Linguistics* (Baltimore, 1955); idem, "Two fundamental problems in phonemics," *Studies in Linguistics* 7.33 (1949); R. Jakobson, "The phonemic and grammatical aspects of language and their interrelation," *Proceedings of the Sixth International Congress of Linguists* 5–18 (Paris, 1948); K. L. Pike, "Grammatical prerequisites to phonemic analysis," *Word* 3.155–72 (1947); idem, "More on grammatical prerequisites," *Word* 8.106–21 (1952), for further discussion on interdependence of levels. Also N. Chomsky, M. Halle, F. Lukoff, "On accent and juncture in English," *For Roman Jakobson* ('s-Gravenhage, 1956), 65–80. '

Bar-Hillel has suggested in "Logical syntax and semantics", *Language* 30.230–7 (1954) that Pike's proposals can be formalized without the circularity

Many problems of morphemic analysis also receive quite simple solutions if we adopt the general framework outlined above. In attempting to develop discovery procedures for grammars we are naturally led to consider morphemes as classes of sequences of phonemes, i.e., as having actual phonemic 'content' in an almost literal sense. This leads to trouble in such well-known cases as English "took" /tuk/, where it is difficult without artificiality to associate any part of this word with the past tense morpheme which appears as /t/ in "walked" /wɔkt/, as /d/ in "framed" /freymd/, etc. We can avoid all such problems by regarding morphology and phonology as two distinct but interdependent levels of representation, related in the grammar by morphophonemic rules such as (19). Thus "took" is represented on the morphological level as *take + past* just as "walked" is represented as *walk + past*. The morphophonemic rules (19 ii), (19 v), respectively, carry these strings of morphemes into /tuk/, /wɔkt/. The only difference between the two cases is that (19 v) is a much more general rule than (19 ii).[8] If we give up the idea that higher levels are literally constructed out of

---

that many sense in them by the use of recursive definitions. He does not pursue this suggestion in any detail, and my own feeling is that success along these lines is unlikely. Moreover, if we are satisfied with an evaluation procedure for grammars, we can construct interdependent levels with only direct definitions, as we have just seen.

The problem of interdependence of phonemic and morphemic levels must not be confused with the question of whether morphological information is required to read a phonemic transcription. Even if morphological considerations are considered relevant to determining the phonemes of a language, it may still be the case that the phonemic transcription provides complete 'reading' rules with no reference to other levels. Cf. N. Chomsky, M. Halle, F. Lukoff, "On accent and juncture in English," *For Roman Jakobson* ('s-Gravenhage, 1956), 65–80, for discussion and examples.

[8]   Hockett gives a very clear presentation of this approach to levels in *A manual of phonology* (1955), p. 15. In "Two models of grammatical description," *Linguistics Today*, *Word* 10.210–33 (1954), Hockett rejected a solution very much like the one we have just proposed on the grounds that "*took* and *take* are partly similar in phonemic shape just as are *baked* and *bake*, and similar in meaning also in the same way; this fact should not be obscured" (p. 224). But the similarity in meaning is not obscured in our formulation, since the morpheme *past* appears in the morphemic representation of both "took" and "baked." And the similarity in phonemic shape can be brought out in the actual

lower level elements, as I think we must, then it becomes much more natural to consider even such abstract systems of representation as transformational structure (where each utterance is represented by the sequence of transformations by which it is derived from a terminal string of the phrase structure grammar) as constituting a linguistic level.

We are not actually forced to give up hope of finding a practical discovery procedure by adopting either the view that levels are interdependent, or the conception of linguistic levels as abstract systems of representation related only by general rules. Nevertheless, I think it is unquestionable that opposition to mixing levels, as well as the idea that each level is literally constructed out of lower level elements, has its origin in the attempt to develop a discovery procedure for grammars. If we renounce this goal and if we distinguish clearly between a manual of suggestive and helpful procedures and a theory of linguistic structure, then there is little reason for maintaining either of these rather dubious positions.

There are many other commonly held views that seem to lose much of their appeal if we formulate our goals in the manner suggested above. Thus it is sometimes argued that work on syntactic theory is premature at this time in view of the fact that many of the problems that arise on the lower levels of phonemics and morphology are unsolved. It is quite true that the higher levels of linguistic description depend on results obtained at the lower levels. But there is also a good sense in which the converse is true. For example, we have seen above that it would be absurd, or even hopeless, to state principles of sentence construction in terms of phonemes or morphemes, but only the development of such higher levels as phrase structure indicates that this futile task need not be

---

formulation of the morphophonemic rule that carries *take + past* into /tuk/. We will no doubt formulate this rules as

ey →u in the context t − k + *past*

in the actual morphophonemic statement. This will allow us to simplify the grammar by a generalization that will bring out the parallel between "take"–"took," "shake"–"shook," "forsake"–"forsook," and more generally, "stand"–"stood," etc.

undertaken on lower levels.[9] Similarly, we have argued that description of sentence structure by constituent analysis will be unsuccessful, if pushed beyond certain limits. But only the development of the still more abstract level of transformations can prepare the way for the development of a simpler and more adequate technique of constituent analysis with narrower limits. The grammar of a language is a complex system with many and varied interconnections between its parts. In order to develop one part of grammar thoroughly, it is often useful, or even necessary, to have some picture of the character of a completed system. Once again, I think that the notion that syntactic theory must await the solution of problems of phonology and morphology is completely untenable whether or not one is concerned with the problem of discovery procedures, but I think it has been nurtured by a faulty analogy between the order of development of linguistic theory and the presumed order of operations in discovery of grammatical structure.

---

[9]   See N. Chomsky, M. Halle, F. Lukoff, "On accent and juncture in English," *For Roman Jakobson* ('s-Gravenhage, 1956), 65–80, for a discussion of the possibility that considerations on all higher levels, including morphology, phrase structure, and transformations, are relevant to the selection of a phonemic analysis.

7

SOME TRANSFORMATIONS IN ENGLISH

7.1 After this digression, we can return to the investigation of the consequences of adopting the transformational approach in the description of English syntax. Our goal is to limit the kernel in such a way that the terminal strings underlying the kernel sentences are derived by a simple system of phrase structure and can provide the basis from which all sentences can be derived by simple transformations: obligatory transformations in the case of the kernel, obligatory *and* optional transformations in the case of non-kernel sentences.

To specify a transformation explicitly we must describe the analysis of the strings to which it applies and the structural change that it effects on these strings.[1] Thus, the passive transformation applies to strings of the form $NP - Aux - V - NP$ and has the effect of interchanging the two noun phrases, adding *by* before the final noun phrase, and adding $be + en$ to *Aux* (Cf. (34)). Consider now the introduction of *not* or *n't* into the auxiliary verb phrase. The simplest way to describe negation is by means of a transformation which applies before (29 ii) and introduces *not* or *n't* after the second morpheme of the phrase given by (28 iii) if this phrase contains at least two morphemes, or after the first morpheme of this phrase if it contains only one. Thus this transformation T_{not} operates on strings that are analyzed into three segments in one of the following ways:

(37) (i) $NP - C - V...$

[1] For a more detailed discussion of the specification of transformations in general and of specific transformations, see the references cited in footnote 8, p. 44.

(ii) $NP - C + M - \ldots$

(iii) $NP - C + have - \ldots$

(iv) $NP - C + be - \ldots$

where the symbols are as in (28), (29), and it is immaterial what stands in place of the dots. Given a string analyzed into three segments in one of these ways, T_{not} adds *not* (or *n't*) after the second segment of the string. For example, applied to the terminal string *they* $\varnothing + can - come$ (an instance of (37ii)), T_{not} gives *they* $- \varnothing + can + n't - come$ (ultimately, "they can't come"); applied to *they* $- \varnothing + have - en + come$ (an instance of (37iii)), it gives *they* $- \varnothing + have + n't - en + come$ (ultimately, "they haven't come"); applied to *they* $- \varnothing + be - ing + come$ (an instance of (37iv)), it gives *they* $- \varnothing + be + n't - ing + come$ (ultimately, "they aren't coming") The rule thus works properly when we select the last three cases of (37).

Suppose, now, that we select an instance of (37i), i e., a terminal string such as

(38) $John - S - come.$

which would give the kernel sentence "John comes" by (29ii). Applied to (38), T_{not} yields

(39) $John - S + n't - come.$

But we specified that T_{not} applies before (29ii), which has the effect of rewriting $Af + v$ as $v + Af \#$. However, we see that (29ii) does not apply at all to (39) since (39) does not now contain a sequence $Af + v$. Let us now add to the grammar the following obligatory transformational rule which applies *after* (29):

(40) $\# Af \rightarrow \# do + Af$

where *do* is the same element as the main verb in "John does his homework". Cf. (29iii) for introduction of $\#$.) What (40) states is that *do* is introduced as the 'bearer' of an unaffixed affix. Applying (40) and morphological rules to (39) we derive "John doesn't come." The rules (37) and (40) now enable us to derive all and only the grammatical forms of sentence negation.

As it stands, the transformational treatment of negation is somewhat simpler than any alternative treatment within phrase structure.

The advantage of the transformational treatment (over inclusion of negatives in the kernel) would become much clearer if we could find other cases in which the same formulations (i.e., (37) and (40)) are required for independent reasons. But in fact there are such cases.

Consider the class of 'yes-or-no' questions such as "have they arrived", "can they arrive," "did they arrive". We can generate all (and only) these sentences by means of a transformation T_q that operates on strings with the analysis (37), and has the effect of interchanging the first and second segments of these strings, as these segments are defined in (37). We require that T_q apply *after* (29i) and *before* (29ii). Applied to

(41) (i) *they* − *O* − *arrive*
   (ii) *they* − *O* + *can* − *arrive*
   (iii) *they* − *O* + *have* − *en* + *arrive*
   (iv) *they* − *O* + *be* − *ing* + *arrive*

which are of the forms (37i − iv), T_q yields the strings

(42) (i) *O* − *they* − *arrive*
   (ii) *O* + *can* − *they* − *arrive*
   (iii) *O* + *have* − *they* − *en* + *arrive*
   (iv) *O* + *be* − *they* − *ing* + *arrive*.

Applying to these the obligatory rules (29ii, iii) and (40), and then the morphophonemic rules, we derive

(43) (i)   do they arrive
   (ii) can they arrive
   (iii) have they arrived
   (iv) are they arriving

in phonemic transcription. Had we applied the obligatory rules directly to (41), with no intervening T_q, we would have derived the sentences

(44) (i)   they arrive
   (ii) they can arrive
   (iii) they have arrived
   (iv) they are arriving.

Thus (43i − iv) are the interrogative counterparts to (44i − iv).

In the case of (42i), *do* is introduced by rule (40) as the bearer of the unaffixed element Ø. If C had been developed into S or *past* by rule (29i), rule (40) would have introduced *do* as a bearer of these elements, and we would have such sentences as "does he arrive," "did he arrive." Note that no new morphophonemic rules are needed to account for the fact that $do + \emptyset \rightarrow$ /duw/, $do + S \rightarrow$ /dəz/, $do + past \rightarrow$ /did/; we need these rules anyway to account for the forms of *do* as a main verb. Notice also that T_q must apply after (29i), or number will not be assigned correctly in questions.

In analyzing the auxiliary verb phrase in rules (28), (29), we considered S to be the morpheme of the third person singular and Ø to be the morpheme affixed to the verb for all other forms of the subject. Thus the verb has S if the noun subject has Ø ("the boy arrives") and the verb has Ø if the subject has S ("the boys arrive"). An alternative that we did not consider was to eliminate the zero morpheme and to state simply that *no* affix occurs if the subject is not third person singular. We see now that this alternative is not acceptable. We must have the Ø morpheme or there will be no affix in (42i) for *do* to bear, and rule (40) will thus not apply to (42i). There are many other cases where transformational analysis provides compelling reasons for or against the establisment of zero morphemes. As a negative case, consider the suggestion that intransitive verbs be analyzed as verbs with zero object. But then the passive transformation (34) would convert, e.g., "John − slept − Ø" into the non-sentence "Ø − was slept − by John" → "was slept by John." Hence this analysis of intransitives must be rejected. We return to the more general problem of the role of transformations in determining constituent structure in § 7.6.

The crucial fact about the question transformation T_q is that almost nothing must be added to the grammar in order to describe it. Since both the subdivision of the sentence that it imposes and the rule for appearance of *do* were required independently for negation, we need only describe the inversion effected by T_q in extending the grammar to account for yes-or-no questions. Putting it differently, transformational analysis brings out the fact that negatives and interrogatives have fundamentally the same 'structure', and it can make use of this fact to simplify the description of English syntax.

In treating the auxiliary verb phrase we left out of consideration forms with the heavy stressed element *do* as in "John *does* come," etc. Suppose we set up a morpheme *A* of contrastive stress to which the following morphophonemic rule applies.

(45) $..V..+A \rightarrow ..\acute{V}..$, where " indicates extra heavy stress.

We now set up a transformation T_A that imposes the same structural analysis of strings as does T_{not} (i.e., (37)), and adds *A* to these strings in exactly the position where T_{not} adds *not* or *n't*. Then just as T_{not} yields such sentences as

(46) (i) John doesn't arrive (from *John # S + n't # arrive*, by (40))

(ii) John can't arrive (from *John # S + can + n't # arrive*)

(iii) John hasn't arrived (from *John # S + have + n't # en + arrive*)

T_A yields the corresponding sentences

(47) (i) John *does* arrive (from *John # S + A # arrive*, by (40))

(ii) John *can* arrive (from *John # S + can + A # arrive*)

(iii) John *has* arrived (from *John # S + have + A # en + arrive*).

Thus T_A is a transformation of 'affirmation' which affirms the sentences "John arrives", "John can arrive", "John has arrived," etc., in exactly the same way as T_{not} negates them. This is formally the simplest solution, and it seems intuitively correct as well.

There are still other instances of transformations that are determined by the same fundamental syntactic analysis of sentences, namely (37). Consider the transformation T_{so} that converts the pairs of strings of (48) into the corresponding strings of (49):

(48) (i)   *John − S − arrive, I − Ø − arrive*

(ii)   *John − S + can − arrive, I − Ø + can − arrive*

(iii)   *John − S + have − en + arrive, I − Ø + have − en + arrive*

(49) (i)   *John − S − arrive − and − so − Ø − I*

(ii)   *John − S + can − arrive − and − so − Ø + can − I*

(iii)   *John − S + have − en + arrive − and − so − Ø + have − I.*

Applying rules (29 ii, iii), (40), and the morphophonemic rules, we ultimately derive

(50) (i)   John arrives and so do I
    (ii)   John can arrive and so can I
    (iii) John has arrived and so have I.

T_{so} operates on the second sentence in each pair in (48), first replacing the third segment of this sentence by *so*, and then interchanging the first and third segment. (The element *so* is thus a pro-VP, in much the same sense in which *he* is a pronoun). The transformation T_{so} combines with the conjunction transformation to give (49). While we have not described this in anywhere near sufficient detail, it is clear that both the analysis (37) of sentences and the rule (40) again are fundamental. Thus almost nothing new is required in the grammar to incorporate such sentences as (50), which are formed on the same underlying transformational pattern as negatives, questions, and emphatic affirmatives.

There is another remarkable indication of the fundamental character of this analysis that deserves mention here. Consider the kernel sentences

(51) (i)   John has a chance to live
    (ii)   John is my friend.

The terminal strings that underly (51) are

(52) (i)   *John + C + have + a + chance + to + live*
    (ii)   *John + C + be + my + friend*

where *have* in (52i) and *be* in (52ii) are main verbs, not auxiliaries. Consider now how the transformations T_{not}, T_q and T_{so} apply to these underlying strings. T_{not} applies to any string of the form (37), adding *not* or *n't* between the second and the third segments, as given in (37). But (52i) is, in fact, an instance of both (37i) and (37iii). Hence T_{not} applied to (52i) will give either (53i) or (53ii):

(53) (i)   *John − C + n't − have + a + chance + to + live*
                (→ "John doesn't have a chance to live")
    (ii)   *John − C + have + n't − a + chance + to + live*
                (→ "John hasn't a chance to live").

But in fact both forms of (53) are grammatical. Furthermore *have* is the only transitive verb for which this ambiguous negation is possible, just as it is the only transitive verb that can be ambiguously analyzed in terms of (37). That is, we have "John doesn't read books" but not "John readsn't books".

Similarly, T_q applied to (52i) will give either form of (54), and T_{so} will give either form of (55), since these transformations are also based on the structural analysis (37).

(54) (i) does John have a chance to live?
     (ii) has John a chance to live?
(55) (i) Bill has a chance to live and so does John.
     (ii) Bill has a chance to live and so has John.

But in the case of all other transitive verbs such forms as (54ii), (55ii) are impossible. We do not have "reads John books?" or "Bill reads books and so reads John". We see, however, that the apparently irregular behavior of "have" is actually an automatic consequence of our rules. This solves the problem raised in § 2.3 concerning the grammaticalness of (3) but not (5).

Now consider (52ii). We have not shown this, but it is in fact true that in the simplest phrase structure grammar of English there is never any reason for incorporating "be" into the class of verbs; i.e., it will not follow from this grammar that *be* is a *V*. Just as one of the forms of the verb phrase is $V + NP$, one of the forms is *be + Predicate*. Hence, even though *be* is not an auxiliary in (52ii), it is nevertheless the case that of the analyses permitted by (37), only (37iv) holds of (52ii). Therefore the transformations T_{not}, T_q, and T_{so}, applied to (52ii), yield, respectively (along with (29i)),

(56) (i)   *John — S + be + n't — my + friend* (→ "John isn't my
                                                     friend")
     (ii) *S + be — John — my + friend* (→ "is John my friend")
     (iii) *Bill — S + be — my + friend — and — so — S + be — John*
                                (→ "Bill is my friend and so is John").

Again, the analogous forms (e.g., "John readsn't books," etc.) are impossible with actual verbs. Similarly, T_A gives "John *is* here" instead of "John *does* be here", as would be the case with actual verbs.

If we were to attempt to describe English syntax wholly in terms

of phrase structure, the forms with "be" and "have" would appear
as glaring and distinct exceptions. But we have just seen that
exactly these apparently exceptional forms result automatically
from the simplest grammar constructed to account for the regular
cases. Hence, this behavior of "be" and "have" actually turns out
to be an instance of a deeper underlying regularity when we consider
English structure from the point of view of transformational analysis.

Notice that the occurrence of *have* as an auxiliary in such terminal
strings as *John + C + have + en + arrive* (underlying the kernel
sentence "John has arrived") is not subject to the same ambiguous
analysis. This terminal string is an instance of (37 iii), but not of
(37 i). That is, it can be analyzed as in (57 i), but not (57 ii).

(57) (i)   *John − C + have − en + arrive* (*NP − C + have −* ..., i.e.,
                                                              (37 iii))
       (ii)   *John − C − have + en + arrive* (*NP − C − V* ..., i.e., (37 i))

This string is not an instance of (37 i) since *this occurrence* of *have* is
not a *V*, even though certain other occurrences of *have* (e.g., in
(52 i)) are *V*'s. The phrase structure of a terminal string is determined from its derivation, by tracing segments back to node points in
the manner described in § 4.1. But *have* in (57) is not traceable to
any node point labelled *V* in the derivation of this string. (52 i) is
ambiguously analyzable, however, since the occurrence of *have* in
(52 i) is traceable back to a *V*, and of course, is traceable back to a
have (namely, itself), in the diagram corresponding to the derivation
of the string (52 i). The fact that (57 ii) is not a permissible analysis
prevents us from deriving such non-sentences as "John doesn't have
arrived", "does John have arrived", etc.

In this section we have seen that a wide variety of apparently
distinct phenomena all fall into place in a very simple and natural
way when we adopt the viewpoint of transformational analysis and
that, consequently, the grammar of English becomes much more
simple and orderly. This is the basic requirement that any conception of linguistic structure (i.e., any model for the form of grammars)
must meet. I think that these considerations give ample justification for our earlier contention that the conceptions of phrase

structure are fundamentally inadequate and that the theory of linguistic structure must be elaborated along the lines suggested in this discussion of transformational analysis.

7.2   We can easily extend the analysis of questions given above to include such interrogatives as

(58) (i)   what did John eat
     (ii)   who ate an apple

which do not receive yes-or-no answers. The simplest way to incorporate this class of sentences into the grammar is by setting up a new optional transformation T_w which operates on any string of the form

(59) $X - NP - Y$

where X and Y stands for any string (including, in particular, the 'null' string — i.e., the first or third position may be empty). T_w then operates in two steps:

(60) (i) T_{w1} converts the string of the form $X - NP - Y$ into the corresponding string of the form $NP - X - Y$; i.e., it inverts the first and second segments of (59). It thus has the same transformational effect as T_q (cf. (41)–(42)).

     (ii) T_{w2} converts the resulting string $NP - X - Y$ into $who - X - Y$ if NP is an animate NP or into $what - X - Y$ if NP is inanimate.[2]

We now require that T_w can apply only to strings to which T_q has already applied. We specified that T_q must apply after (29i) and before (29ii). T_w applies after T_q and before (29ii), and it is conditional upon T_q in the sense that it can only apply to forms given by T_q. This conditional dependence among transformations is a generalization of the distinction between obligatory and optional transformations which we can easily build into the grammar, and

---

[2]   More simply, we can limit application of T_w to strings $X - NP - Y$ where NP is *he*, *him*, or *it*, and we can define T_{w2} as the transformation that converts any string Z into $wh + Z$, where *wh* is a morpheme. In the morphophonemics of English we shall have rules: $wh + he \rightarrow$ /huw/, $wh + him \rightarrow$ /huwm/, $wh + it \rightarrow$ /wat/.

which proves essential. The terminal string underlying both (58 i) and (58 ii) (as well as (62), (64)) is

(61)   *John − C − eat + an + apple (NP − C − V ...)*,

where the dashes indicate the analysis imposed by T_q. Thus (61) is a case of (37 i), as indicated. If we were to apply only obligatory transformations to (61), choosing *past* in developing *C* by (29 i), we would derive

(62)   # *John* # *eat + past* # *an* # *apple* # (→ "John ate an apple")

If we apply (29 i) and T_q to (61), we derive

(63)   *past − John − eat + an + apple,*

where *C* is taken as *past*. If we were now to apply (40) to (63), introducing *do* as the bearer of *past*, we would have the simple interrogative

(64)   did John eat an apple

If we apply T_w to (63), however, we derive first (65), by T_{w1}, and then (66), by T_{w2}.

(65)   *John − past − eat + an + apple*
(66)   *who − past − eat + an + apple.*

Rule (29 ii) and the morphophonemic rules then convert (66) into (58 ii). To form (58 ii), then, we apply first T_q and then T_w to the terminal string (61) that underlies the kernel sentence (62). Note that in this case T_{w1} simply undoes the effect of T_q, which explains the absence of inversion in (58 ii).

To apply T_w to a string, we first select a noun phrase and then invert this noun phrase with the string that precedes it. In forming (58 ii), we applied T_w to (63), choosing the noun phrase *John*. Suppose now that we apply T_w to (63), choosing the noun phrase *an + apple*. Thus for the purposes of this transformation we now analyze (63) as

(67)   *past + John + eat − an + apple,*

a string of the form (59), where *Y* in this case is null. Applying T_w to (67) we derive first (68), by T_{w1}, and then (69), by T_{w2}.

(68)   *an + apple − past + John + eat*

(69) *what — past + John + eat.*

(29ii) does not now apply to (69), just as it did not apply to (39) or (42i), since (69) does not contain a substring of the form $Af + v$. Hence (40) applies to (69), introducing *do* as a bearer of the morpheme *past*. Applying the remaining rules, we finally derive (58i).

T_w as formulated in (59)–(60) will also account for all such *wh*-questions as "what will he eat", "what has he been eating". It can easily be extended to cover interrogatives like "what book did he read", etc.

Notice that T_{w1} as defined in (60i) carries out the same transformation as does T_q; that is, it inverts the first two segments of the string to which it applies. We have not discussed the effect of transformations on intonation. Suppose that we set up two fundamental sentence intonations: falling intonations, which we associate with kernel sentences, and rising intonations, which we associate with yes-or-no questions. Then the effect of T_q is in part to convert the intonation from one of these to the other; hence, in the case of (64), to convert a falling intonation into a rising one. But we have seen that T_{w1} applies only after T_q, and that its transformational effect is the same as that of T_q. Hence T_{w1} will convert the rising intonation back into a falling one. It seems reasonable to put this forth as an explanation for the fact that the interrogatives (58i-ii) normally have the falling intonation of declaratives. There are many problems in extending our discussion to intonational phenomena and this remark is too sketchy to carry much weight, but it does suggest that such an extension may be fruitful.

To summarize, we see that the four sentences

(70) (i)   John ate an apple $(= (62))$
     (ii) did John eat an apple $(= (64))$
     (iii) what did John eat $(= (58i))$
     (iv) who ate an apple $(= (58ii))$

are all derived from the underlying terminal string (61). (70i) is a kernel sentence, since only obligatory transformations enter into its 'transformational history.' (70ii) is formed from (61) by applying

T_q. (70iii) and (70iv) are even more remote from the kernel, since they are formed from (61) by applying first T_q and then T_w. We shall refer to this analysis briefly in § 8.2.

7.3 In § 5.3 we mentioned that there are certain noun phrases of the form *to* + *VP*, *ing* + *VP* ("to prove that theorem," "proving that theorem"— cf. (32)–(33)). Among these we will have such phrases as "to be cheated," "being cheated", which are derived from passives. But passives have been deleted from the kernel. Hence noun phrases of the type *to* + *VP*, *ing* + *NP* can no longer be introduced within the kernel grammar by such rules as (33). They must therefore be introduced by a 'nominalizing transformation' which converts a sentence of the form *NP* − *VP* into a noun phrase of the form *to* + *VP* or *ing* + *VP*.[3] We shall not go into the structure of this very interesting and ramified set of nominalizing transformations except to sketch briefly a transformational explanation for a problem raised in § 2.3.

One of the nominalizing transformations will be the transformation T_{adj} which operates on any string of the form

(71) $T - N - is - Adj$ (i.e., article − noun − is − adjective)

and converts it into the corresponding noun phrase of the form $T + Adj + N$. Thus, it converts "the boy is tall" into "the tall boy," etc. It is not difficult to show that this transformation simplifies the grammar considerably, and that it must go in this, not the opposite direction. When we formulate this transformation properly, we find that it enables us to drop all adjective-noun combinations from the kernel, reintroducing them by T_{Adj}.

In the phrase structure grammar we have a rule

(72) *Adj → old, tall, ...*

---

[3] This nominalizing transformation will be given as a generalized transformation such as (26). It will operate on a pair sentences, one of which it converts from *NP* − *VP* into *to* + *VP* (or *ing* + *VP*), which it then substitutes for an *NP* of the other sentence. See my *The logical structure of linguistic theory* and *Transformational analysis* for a detailed discussion. – For a fuller and more adequate analysis of the material in this subsection, see my "A transformational approach to syntax," *Proceedings of the University of Texas Symposium of 1958* (to appear).

which lists all of the elements that can occur in the kernel sentences of the form (71). Words like "sleeping", however, will not be given in this list, even though we have such sentences as

(73) the child is sleeping.

The reason for this is that even when "sleeping" is not listed in (72), (73) is generate by the transformation (29 ii) (that carries $Af + v$ into $v + Af \#$) form the underlying terminal string

(74) $the + child + C + be - ing - sleep,$

where $be + ing$ is part of the auxiliary verb (cf. (28 iii)). Alongside of (73), we have such sentences as "the child will sleep," "the child sleeps," etc., with different choices for the auxiliary verb.

Such words as "interesting", however, will have to be given in the list (73). In such sentences as

(75) the book is interesting,

"interesting" is an Adj, not part of the $Verb$, as can be seen from the fact that we do not have "the book will interest," "the book interests," etc.

An independent support for this analysis of "interesting" and "sleeping" comes from the behavior of "very," etc., which can occur with certain adjectives, but not others. The simplest way to account for "very" is to put into the phrase structure grammar the rule

(76) $Adj \rightarrow very + Adj.$

"very" can appear in (75), and in general with "interesting"; but it cannot appear in (73) or with other occurrences of "sleeping." Hence, if we wish to preserve the simplest analysis of "very," we must list "interesting" but not "sleeping" in (72) as an Adj.

We have not discussed the manner in which transformations impose constituent structure, although we have indicated that this is necessary; in particular, so that transformations can be compounded. One of the general conditions on derived constituent structure will be the following:

(77) If X is a Z in the phrase structure grammar, and a string Y formed by a transformation is of the same structural form as X, then Y is also a Z.

In particular, even when passives are deleted from the kernel we will want to say that the *by*-phrase (as in "the food was eaten — by the man") is a prepositional phrase (*PP*) in the passive sentence. (77) permits this, since we know from the kernel grammar that $by + NP$ is a *PP*. (77) is not stated with sufficient accuracy, but it can be elaborated as one of a set of conditions on derived constituent structure.

But now consider (73). The word "sleeping" is formed by transformation (i.e., (29ii)) and it is of the same form as "interesting" (i.e., it is a $V + ing$), which, as we know from the phrase structure grammar, is an *Adj*. Hence, by (77), "sleeping" is also an *Adj* in the transform (73). But this means that (73) can be analyzed as a string of the form (71) so that T_{Adj} applies to it, forming the noun phrase

(78)   the sleeping child

just as it forms "the interesting book" from (75). Thus even though "sleeping" is excluded from (72), it will appear as an adjective modifying nouns.

This analysis of adjectives (which is all that we are required to give to account for the actually occurring sentences) will not introduce the word "sleeping," however, into all the adjective positions of such words as "interesting" which remained in the kernel. For example, it will never introduce "sleeping" into the context "very —." Since "very" never modifies verbs, "very" will not appear in (74) or (73), and all occurences of "sleeping" as a modifier are derived from its occurrence as a verb in (74), etc. Similarly, there will be phrase structure rules that analyze the verb phrase into

(79) $Aux + seem + Adj$

just as other rules analyze *VP* into $Aux + V + NP$, $Aux + be + Adj$. etc. But "sleeping" will never be introduced into the context "seems —" by this grammar, which is apparently the simplest one constructible for the actually occurring sentences.

When we develop this sketchy argument more carefully, we reach the conclusion that the simplest transformational grammar for the occurring sentences will exclude (80) while generating (81).

(80) (i)   the child seems sleeping
     (ii)   the very sleeping child
(81) (i)   the book seems interesting
     (ii)   the very interesting book.

We see, then, that the apparently arbitrary distinctions noted in § 2.3 between (3) (= "have you a book on modern music?") and (4) (= (81 i)) on the one hand, and (5) (= "read you a book on modern music?") and (6) (= (80 i)) on the other, have a clear structural origin, and are really instances of higher level regularity in the sense that they are consequences of the simplest transformational grammar.   In other words, certain linguistic behavior that seems unmotivated and inexplicable in terms of phrase structure appears simple and systematic when we adopt the transformational point of view.   To use the terminology of § 2.2, if a speaker were to project his finite linguistic experience by using phrase structure and transformations in the simplest possible way, consistent with his experience, he would include (3) and (4) as grammatical while rejecting (5) and (6).

7.4   In (28), § 5.3, we analyzed the element *Verb* into *Aux* + *V*, and then simply listed the verbal roots of the class *V*.   There are, however, a large number of productive subscontructions of *V* that deserve some mention, since they bring to light some basic points in a rather clear way.   Consider first such verb + particle ($V + Prt$) constructions as "bring in," "call up," "drive away."   We can have such forms as (82) but not (83).

(82) (i)   the police brought in the criminal
     (ii)   the police brought the criminal in
     (iii)   the police brought him in
(83)   the police brought in him.

We know that discontinuous elements cannot be handled readily within the phrase structure grammar.   Hence the most natural way of analyzing these constructions is to add to (28 ii) the following possibility:

(84) $V \rightarrow V_1 + Prt$

along with a set of supplementary rules to indicate which V_1 can go with which *Prt*. To allow for the possibility of (82ii) we set up an optional transformation T^{op}_{sep} which operates on strings with the structural analysis

(85) $X - V_1 - Prt - NP$

and has the effect of interchanging the third and fourth segments of the string to which it applies. It thus carries (82i) into (82ii). To provide for (82iii) while excluding (83), we must indicate that this transformation is obligatory when the *NP* object is a pronoun (*Pron*). Equivalently, we can set up an obligatory transformation T^{ob}_{sep} which has the same structural effect as T^{op}_{sep} but which operates on strings with the structural analysis

(86) $X - V_1 - Prt - Pron$

We know that the passive transformation operates on any string of the form $NP - Verb - NP$. If we specify that the passive transformation applies before T^{op}_{sep} or T^{ob}_{sep}, then it will form the passives

(87) (i)   the criminal was brought in by the police

    (ii)   he was brought in by the police

from (82), as it should.

    Further investigation of the verb phrase shows that there is a general verb + complement ($V + Comp$) construction that behaves very much like the verb + particle construction just discussed. Consider the sentences

(88)   everyone in the lab considers John incompetent

(89)   John is considered incompetent by everyone in the lab.

If we wish to derive (89) from (88) by the passive transformation we must analyze (88) into the structure $NP_1 - Verb - NP_2$, where $NP_1 = everyone + in + the + lab$ and $NP_2 = John$. That is, we must apply the passive not to (88), but to a terminal string (90) that underlies (88):

(90)   everyone in the lab − considers incompetent − John.

We can now form (88) from (90) by a transformation analogous to T^{ob}_{sep}. Suppose that we add to the phrase structure grammar the rule (91), alongside (84).

(91) $V \rightarrow V_a + Comp$

We now extend T_{sep}^{ob} permitting it to apply to strings of the form (92) as well as to strings of the form (86), as before.

(92) $X - V_a - Comp - NP$.

This revised transformation T_{sep}^{ob} will convert (90) into (88). Thus, the treatment of the verb + complement and verb + particle constructions are quite similar. The former, in particular, is an extremely well-developed construction in English.[4]

7.5   We have barely sketched the justification for the particular form of each of the transformations that we have discussed, though it is very important to study the question of the uniqueness of this system. I think it can be shown that in each of the cases considered above, and in many other cases, there are very clear and easily generalizable considerations of simplicity that determine which set of sentences belong to the kernel and what sorts of transformations are required to account for the non-kernel sentences. As a paradigmatic instance, we shall briefly review the status of the passive transformation.

In § 5.4 we showed that the grammar is much more complex if it contains both actives and passives in the kernel than if the passives are deleted and reintroduced by a transformation that interchanges the subject and object of the active, and replaces the verb V by $is + V + en + by$. Two questions about uniqueness immediately suggest themselves. First, we ask whether it is necessary to inter-

---

[4]   Further study shows that most of the verb + complement forms introduced by rule (91) should themselves be excluded from the kernel and derived transformationally from "John is incompetent," etc. But this is a complex matter that requires a much more detailed development of transformational theory than we can give here. Cf. my *The logical structure of linguistic theory, Transformational analysis* and "A transformational approach to syntax".

There are several other features of these constructions that we have passed over far too briefly. It is not at all clear that this is an obligatory transformation. With long and complex objects we can have, e.g., "they consider incompetent anyone who is unable to..." Hence we might extend T_{sep}^{op}, rather than T_{sep}^{ob}, to take care of this case. It is interesting to study those features of the grammatical object that necessitate or preclude this transformation. Much more than length is involved. There are also other possibilities for the passive that we shall not consider here, for lack of space, though they make an interesting study.

change the noun phrases to form the passive. Second, we ask whether passives could have been chosen as the kernel, and actives derived from them by an 'active' transformation.

Consider first the question of the interchange of subject and object. Is this interchange necessary, or could we describe the passive transformation as having the following effect:

(93)　$NP_1 - Aux - V - NP_2$ is rewritten $NP_1 - Aux + be + en - V - by + NP_2$.

In particular, the passive of "John loves Mary" would be "John is loved by Mary."

In § 5.4 we argued against (93) and in favor of inversion on the basis of the fact that we have such sentences as (94) but not (95).

(94) (i)　John admires sincerity　— sincerity is admired by John
　　 (ii)　John plays golf　　　　　 — golf is played by John
　　 (iii)　sincerity frightens John — John is frightened by sincerity
(95) (i)　sincerity admires John　 — John is admired by sincerity
　　 (ii)　golf plays John　　　　　 — John is played by golf
　　 (iii)　John frightens sincerity — sincerity is frightened by John.

We pointed out, however, that this approach requires that a notion of "degree of grammaticalness" be developed to support this distinction. I believe that this approach is correct, and that there is a clear sense in which the sentences of (94) are more grammatical than those of (95), which are themselves more grammatical than "sincerity admires eat," etc. Any grammar that distinguishes abstract from proper nouns would be subtle enough to characterize the difference between (94 i, iii) and (95 i, iii), for example, and surely linguistic theory must provide the means for this distinction. However, since we have not gone into the question of category analysis in this discussion, it is interesting to show that there is even a stronger argument against (93). In fact, any grammar that can distinguish singular from plural is sufficiently powerful to enable us to prove that the passive requires inversion of noun phrases.

To see this, consider the verb + complement construction discussed in § 7.4. Alongside (88), (89) we have such sentences as:

(96) all the people in the lab consider John a fool

(97) John is considered a fool by all the people in the lab.

In § 7.4 we saw that (96) is formed by the transformation T_{sep}^{ob} from the underlying string

(98) all the people in the lab – consider a fool – John (NP – $Verb$ – NP).

with the $Verb$ "consider a fool" being an instance of (91). We also saw that the passive transformation applies directly to (98). If the passive interchanges subject and object, it will correctly form (97) from (98) as the passive of (96). If, however, we take (93) as the definition of the passive, we will derive the non-sentence.

(99) all the people in the lab are considered a fool by John

by application of this transformation to (98).

The point is that we have found a verb — namely, "consider a fool" — which must agree in number both with its subject and its object.[5] Such verbs prove quite conclusively that the passive must be based on an inversion of subject and object.

Consider now the question of whether passives could be taken as the kernel sentences instead of actives. It is quite easy to see that this proposal leads to a much more complex grammar. With actives as kernel sentences, the phrase structure grammar will include (28) with $be + en$ dropped from (28 iii). But if passives are taken as kernel sentences, $be + en$ will have to be listed in (28 iii), along with all the other forms of the auxiliary, and we will have to add special rules indicating that if V is intransitive, it cannot have the auxiliary $be + en$ (i.e., we cannot have "is occurred"), whereas if V is transitive it must have $be + en$ (i.e., we cannot have "lunch eats by John"). Comparing the two alternatives, there is no doubt as to relative complexity; and we are forced to take actives, not passives, as the kernel sentences.

Notice that if passives were chosen as kernel sentences instead of actives we would run into certain difficulties of quite a different sort.

---

[5] The agreement between "a fool" and "John" in (98) is of course one support for the futher transformational analysis of the verb + complement + noun phrase constructions mentioned in footnote 4 on p. 77.

The active transformation would have to apply to strings of the form

(100) $NP_1 - Aux + be + en - V - by + NP_2$,

converting them to $NP_2 - Aux - V - NP_1$. For example, it would convert

(101)   the wine was drunk by the guests

into "the guests drank the wine," where "drunk" in (101) originates from $en + drink$. But there is also an adjective "drunk" that must be listed in (72) along with "old," "interesting," etc., since we have "he is very drunk," "he seems drunk," etc. (cf. § 7.3), and this adjective will also originate from $en + drink$. It thus appears that in the simplest system of phrase structure for English, the sentence

(102)   John was drunk by midnight

is also based on an underlying terminal string that can be analyzed in accordance with (100). In other words, there is no structural way to differentiate properly between (101) and (102), if both are taken as kernel sentences. But application of the 'active' transformation to (102) does not give a grammatical sentence.

When we actually try to set up, for English, the simplest grammar that contains a phrase structure and transformational part, we find that the kernel consist of simple, declarative, active sentences (in fact, probably a finite number of these), and that all other sentences can be described more simply as transforms. Each transformation that I have investigated can be shown to be irreversible in the sense that it is much easier to carry out the transformation in one direction than in the other, just as in the case of the passive transformation discussed above. This fact may account for the traditional practice of grammarians, who customarily begin the grammar of English, for example, with the study of simple 'actor-action' sentences and simple grammatical relations such as subject-predicate or verb-object. No one would seriously begin the study of English constituent structure with such a sentence as "whom have they nominated," attempting to analyze it into two parts, etc.; and while some very detailed considerations of English structure (e.g., reference [33]) do not mention interrogatives, none fails to include simple declaratives. Transformational analysis provides a rather simple explanation for this assymmetry (which is otherwise formally unmotivated) on the assumption that grammarians have been acting on the basis of a correct intuition about the language.[6]

7.6 One other point deserves some mention before we leave the topic of English transformations. At the outset of § 5 we noted that the rule for conjunction provides a useful criterion for constituent analysis in the sense that this rule is greatly simplified if constituents are set up in a certain way. Now we are interpreting this rule as a transformation. There are many other cases in which the behavior of a sentence under transformations provides valuable, even compelling evidence as to its constituent structure.

Consider for example the pair of sentences

(103) (i) John knew the boy studying in the library.

(ii) John found the boy studying in the library.

It is intuitively obvious that these sentences have different grammatical structure (this becomes clear, for example, when we attempt to add "not running around in the streets" to (103)), but I do not believe that within the level of phrase structure grounds can be found for analyzing them into different constituents. The simplest analysis in both cases is as $NP - Verb - NP - ing + VP$. But consider the behavior of these sentences under the passive transformation. We have the sentences (104) but not (105).[7]

---

[6] In determining which of two related forms is more central, we are thus following the reasoning outlined by Bloomfield for morphology: "...when forms are partially similar, there may be a question as to which one we had better take as the underlying form... the structure of the language may decide this question for us, since, taking it one way, we get an unduly complicated description, and taking it the other way, a relatively simple one," (*Language* [New York, 1933], p. 218). Bloomfield continues by pointing out that "this same consideration often leads us to *set up* an artificial underlying form." We have also found this insight useful in transformational analysis, as, e.g., when we set up the terminal string *John — C — have + en — be + ing — read* underlying the kernel sentence "John has been reading."

[7] The sentences of (104) without the parenthesized expression are formed by a second 'elliptical' transformation that converts e.g., "the boy was seen by John" into "the boy was seen."

(104) (i) the boy studying in the library was known (by John)
     (ii) the boy studying in the library was found (by John)
    (iii) the boy was found studying in the library (by John)
(105) the boy was known studying in the library (by John)

The passive transformation applies only to sentences of the form $NP - Verb - NP$. Hence, to yield (104 ii), (103 ii) must be analyzable as

(106) John − found − the boy studying in the library,

with the noun phrase object "the boy studying in the library," (103 i) will have a corresponding analysis, since we have the passive (104 i).

But (103 ii) also has the passive (104 iii). From this we learn that (103 ii) is a case of the verb + complement construction studied in § 7.4; i.e., that it is derived by the transformation T_{sep}^{ob} from the underlying string

(107) John − found studying in the library − the boy,

with the verb "found" and the complement "studying in the library." The passive transformation will convert (107) into (104 iii), just as it converts (90) into (89). (103 i), however, is not a transform of the string "John − knew studying in the library − the boy" (the same form as (107)), since (105) is not a grammatical sentence.

By studying the grammatical passives, then, we determine that "John found the boy studying in the library" (= (103 ii) is analyzable ambiguously as either $NP - Verb - NP$, with the object "the boy studying in the library," or as $NP - Aux + V - NP - Comp$, a transform of the string (107 which has the complex $Verb$ "found studying in the library." "John knew the boy studying in the library" (= (103 i)), however, has only the first of these analyses. The resulting description of (103) seems quite in accord with intuition.

As another example of a similar type, consider the sentence

(108) John came home.

Although "John" and "home" are NP's, and "came" is a *Verb*, investigation of the effect of transformations on (108) shows that it cannot be analyzed as a case of *NP − Verb − NP*. We cannot have "home was come by John" under the passive transformation, or "what did John come" under the question transformation T_w. We must therefore analyze (108) in some other way (if we are not to complicate unduly the description of these transformations), perhaps as *NP − Verb − Adverb*. Apart from such considerations as these, there do not appear to be very strong reasons for denying to (108) the completely counterintuitive analysis *NP − Verb − NP*, with "home" the object of "came".

I think it is fair to say that a significant number of the basic criteria for determining constituent structure are actually trans-formational. The general principle is this: if we have a transform-ation that simplifies the grammar and leads from sentences to sentences in a large number of cases (i.e., a transformation under which the set of grammatical sentences is very nearly closed), then we attempt to assign constituent structure to sentences in such a way that this transformation always leads to grammatical sentences, thus simplifying the grammar even further.

The reader will perhaps have noted a certain circularity or even apparent inconsistency in our approach. We define such trans-formations as the passive in terms of particular phrase structure analyses, and we then consider the behavior of sentences under these transformations in determining how to assign phrase structure to these sentences. In § 7.5 we used the fact that "John was drunk by midnight" (=(102)) does not have a corresponding 'active' as an argument against setting up a passive-to-active transformation. In § 7.6 we have used the fact that "John came home" (=(108)) does not have a passive as an argument against assigning to it the con-stituent structure *NP − Verb − NP*. However, if the argument is traced carefully in each case it will be clear that there is no circularity or inconsistency. In each case our sole concern has been to decrease the complexity of the grammar, and we have tried to show that the proposed analysis is clearly simpler than the rejected alternatives. In some cases the grammar becomes simpler if we reject a certain transformation: in some cases reassignment of constituent structure is preferable. We have thus been following the course outlined in § 6. Making use of phrase structure and transformations, we are trying to construct a grammar of English that will be simpler than any proposed alternative; and we are giving no thought to the question of how one might actually arrive at this grammar in some mechanical way from an English corpus, no matter how extensive. Our weaker goal of evaluation instead of discovery eliminates any fear of vicious circularity in the cases discussed above. The intuitive correspondences and explanations of apparent irregularities seem to me to offer important evidence for the correctness of the approach we have been following. Cf. § 8.

8

THE EXPLANATORY POWER OF LINGUISTIC
THEORY

8.1 So far we have considered the linguist's task to be that of producing a device of some sort (called a grammar) for generating all and only the sentences of a language, which we have assumed were somehow given in advance. We have seen that this conception of the linguist's activities leads us naturally to describe languages in terms of a set of levels of representation, some of which are quite abstract and non-trivial. In particular, it leads us to establish phrase structure and transformational structure as distinct levels of representation for grammatical sentences. We shall now proceed to formulate the linguist's goals in quite different and independent terms which, however, lead to very similar notions of linguistic structure.

There are many facts about language and linguistic behavior that require explanation beyond the fact that such and such a string (which no one may ever have produced) is or is not a sentence. It is reasonable to expect grammars to provide explanations for some of these facts. For example, for many English speakers the phoneme sequence /əneym/ can be understood ambiguously as either "a name" or "an aim". If our grammar were a one-level system dealing only with phonemes, we would have no explanation for this fact. But when we develop the level of morphological representation, we find that, for quite independent reasons, we are forced to set up morphemes "a", "an", "aim" and "name", associated with the phonemic shapes /ə/, /ən/, /eym/ and /neym/. Hence, as an automatic consequence of the attempt to set up the morphology in the simplest possible way we find that the phoneme sequence /əneym/ is ambiguously represented on the morphological level. In general,

86 SYNTACTIC STRUCTURES

we say that we have a case of *constructional homonymity* when a certain phoneme sequence is analyzed in more than one way on some level. This suggests a criterion of adequacy for grammars We can test the adequacy of a given grammar by asking whether or not each case of constructional homonymity is a real case of ambiguity and each case of the proper kind of ambiguity is actually a case of constructional homonymity.[1] More generally, if a certain conception of the form of grammar leads to a grammar of a given language that fails this test, we may question the adequacy of this conception and the linguistic theory that underlies it. Thus, a perfectly good argument for the establishment of a level of morphology is that this will account for the otherwise unexplained ambiguity of /əneym/.

We have a case of constructional homonymity when some phoneme sequence is ambiguously represented. Suppose that on some level two distinct phoneme sequences are similarly or identically analyzed. We expect that these sequences should somehow be 'understood' in a similar manner, just as cases of dual representation are 'understood' in more than one way. For example, the sentences

(109) (i)   John played tennis
      (ii) my friend likes music

are quite distinct on phonemic and morphemic levels. But on the level of phrase structure they are both represented as $NP - Verb - NP$; correspondingly, it is evident that in some sense they are similarly understood. This fact could not be explained in terms of a grammar that did not go beyond the level words or morphemes, and such instances offer a motivation for establishing the level of phrase structure that is quite independent of that advanced in § 3. Note that considerations of structural ambiguity can also be brought

[1] Obviously, not all kinds of ambiguity will be analyzable in syntactic terms. For example, we would not expect a grammar to explain the referential ambiguity of "son"–"sun", "light" (in color, weight), etc.

In his "Two models of grammatical description," *Linguistics Today, Word* 10.210–33 (1954), Hockett uses notions of structural ambiguity to demonstrate the independence of various linguistic notions in a manner very similar to what we are suggesting here.

forth as a motivation for establishing a level of phrase structure. Such expressions as "old men and women" and "they are flying planes" (i.e., "those specks on the horizon are ...", "my friends are ...") are evidently ambiguous, and in fact they are ambiguously analyzed on the level of phrase structure, though not on any lower level. Recall that the analysis of an expression on the level of phrase structure is provided not by a single string but by a diagram such as (15) or, equivalently, by a certain *set* of representing strings.[2]

What we are suggesting is that the notion of "understanding a sentence" be explained in part in terms of the notion of "linguistic level". To understand a sentence, then, it is first necessary to reconstruct its analysis on each linguistic level; and we can test the adequacy of a given set of abstract linguistic levels by asking whether or not grammars formulated in terms of these levels enable us to provide a satisfactory analysis of the notion of "understanding." Cases of higher level similarity of representation and higher level dissimilarity (constructional homonymity) are simply the extreme cases which, if this framework is accepted, prove the existence of higher levels. In general, we cannot understand any sentence fully unless we know at least how it is analyzed on all levels, including such higher levels as phrase structure, and, as we shall see, transformational structure.

We were able to show the inadequacy of a theory of linguistic structure that stopped short of phrase structure by exhibiting c ases of ambiguity and similarity of understanding that were unexplained on lower levels. But it turns out that there is still a large residue of unexplained cases even after the level of phrase structure is established and applied to English. Analysis of these cases demonstrates the

---

[2]   That is, by what is called a "phrase marker" in my *The logical structure of linguistic theory* and "Three models for the description of language" (above, p. 22, fn. 1). See "Three models..." for discussion of the constructional homonymity of "they are flying planes" within a phrase structure grammar. When we adjoin a transformational grammar to the phrase structure grammar, this sentence is, however, an example of transformational ambiguity, not constructional homonymity within phrase structure. In fact, it is not clear that there are *any* cases of constructional homonymity purely within the level of phrase structure once a transformational grammar is developed.

necessity for a still 'higher' level of transformational analysis in a manner independent of §§ 5, 7. I shall mention only a few representative instances.

8.2   In § 7.6 we came across ar example of a sentence (i.e., "I found the boy studying in the library" = (103 ii)) whose ambiguity of representation could not be demonstrated without bringing transformational criteria to bear. We found that under one interpretation this sentence was a transform under T^{ob}_{sep} of "I − found studying in the library — the boy," and that under another interpretation it was analyzed into an $NP - Verb - NP$ construction with the object "the boy studying in the library." Further transformational analysis would show that in both cases the sentence is a transform of the pair of terminal strings that underlie the simple kernel sentences

(110) (i)   I found the boy
      (ii)   the boy is studying in the library.

Hence this is an interesting case of a sentence whose ambiguity is the result of alternative transformational developments from the same kernel strings. This is quite a complicated example, however, requiring a fairly detailed study of the way in which transformations assign constituent structure, and simpler examples of ambiguity with a transformational origin are not hard to find.

Consider the phrase (111), which can be understood ambiguously with "hunters" as the subject, analogously to (112i), or as the object, analogously to (112ii).

(111)   the shooting of the hunters
(112) (i)   the growling of lions
      (ii)   the raising of flowers.

On the level of phrase structure there is no good way to explain this ambiguity; all of these phrases are represented as *the − V + ing − of + NP*.[3] In transformational terms, however, there is a clear and

---

[3]   It is true that (111) may be represented ambiguously with *shoot* taken either as a transitive or an intransitive verb, but the essential fact here is that the

automatic explanation. Careful analysis of English shows that we can simplify the grammar if we strike such phrases as (111) and (112) out of the kernel and reintroduce them by transformation. To account for such phrases as (112i), we will set up a transformation that carries any sentence of the form $NP - C - V$ into the corresponding phrase of the form $the - V + ing - of + NP$; and this transformation will be designed in such a way that the result is an NP.[4] To account for (112ii), we will set up a transformation which carries any sentence of the form $NP_1 - C - V - NP_2$ into the corresponding NP of the form $the - V + ing - of + NP_2$. Thus the first of these transformations will carry "lions growl" into "the growling of lions," and the second will carry "John raises flowers" into "the raising of flowers." But both "the hunters shoot" and "they shoot the hunters" are kernel sentences. Hence (111) = "the shooting of the hunters" will have two distinct transformational origins; it will be ambiguously represented on the transformational level. The ambiguity of the grammatical relation in (111) is a consequence of the fact that the relation of "shoot" to "hunters" differs in the two underlying kernel sentences. We do not have this ambiguity in (112), since neither "they growl lions" nor "flowers raise" are grammatical kernel sentences.

Similarly, consider such pairs as

(113) (i)   the picture was painted by a new technique
     (ii) the picture was painted by a real artist.

These sentences are understood quite differently, though identically represented as $NP - was + Verb + en - by + NP$ on the level of phrase structure. But their transformational history is quite different. (113ii) is the passive of "a real artist painted the picture". (113i) is

---

grammatical relation in (111) is ambiguous (i.e., "hunters" may be subject or object). Grammatical relations can be defined within phrase structure in terms of the shape of the diagrams (15), etc. But in these terms there will be no grounds for the assertion that *either* the subject-verb *or* the verb-object relation is to be found in (111) If we analyze verbs into three classes, transitive, intransitive and either transitive or intransitive, then even this (in itself insufficient) distinction disappears.

4   Cf. footnote 3 on p. 72.

formed from, e.g., "John painted the picture by a new technique" by a double transformation; first the passive, then the elliptical transformation (mentioned in fn. 7 on p. 81) that drops the 'agent' in the passive. An absolute homonym on the model of (113) is not hard to find. For example,

(114)   John was frightened by the new methods.

may mean either that John is a conservative — new methods frighten him; or that new methods of frightening people were used to frighten John (an interpretation that would be the more normal one if "being" were inserted after "was"). On the transformational level, (114) has both the analysis of (113i) and (113ii), which accounts for its ambiguity.

8.3   We can complete the argument by presenting an example of the opposite extreme; namely, a case of sentences which are understood in a similar manner, though they are quite distinct in phrase structure and lower level representation. Consider the following sentences, discussed in § 7.2.

(115) (i) John ate an apple   — declarative
      (ii) did John eat an apple— yes-or-no-question ⎱
      (iii) what did John eat   ⎱   ⎰ interrogative
      (iv) who ate an apple   ⎰ − *wh*-question   ⎰

It is intuitively obvious that (115) contains two types of sentences, declaratives (115i) and interrogatives (115ii–iv). Furthermore, the interrogatives are intuitively subdivided into two types, the yes-or-no-question (115ii), and the *wh*-questions (115iii, iv). It is difficult, however, to find a formal basis for this classification that is not arbitrary and *ad hoc*. If, for example, we classify sentences by their 'normal' intonation, then (115i), (115iii) and (115iv), with the normal declarative (falling) intonation, will be opposed to (115ii), with rising intonation. If we classify sentences on the basis of word order, then (115i) and (115iv), with normal $NP - Verb - NP$ order, will be opposed to (115ii) and (115iii), which have inversion of subject and auxiliary. Nevertheless, any grammar of English will classify these sentences in the manner indicated in (115), and any speaker of English will understand these sentences according to this pattern. Certainly a linguistic theory that fails to provide grounds for this classification must be judged inadequate.

The representation of a string on the level of transformations is given by the terminal string (or strings) form which it originates and the sequence of transformations by which it is derived from this underlying string. In §§ 7.1–2 we came to the following conclusions about the sentences (115) (= (70)). Each of these sentences originates from the underlying terminal string.

(116)   *John C − eat + an + apple* (= (61)),

which is derived within the phrase structure grammar. (115i) is derived from (116) by applying obligatory transformations only; hence, it is by definition a kernel sentence. (115ii) is formed from (116) by applying the obligatory transformations and T_q. Both (115iii) and (115iv) are formed by applying obligatory transformations, T_q, and T_w. They differ from one another only in the choice of the noun phrase to which T_w applies. Suppose that we determine sentence types in general in terms of transformational history, i.e., representation on the transformational level. Then the major subdivisions of (115) are the kernel sentence (115i) on the one hand, and (115ii–iv), all of which have T_q in their transformational representation, on the other. Thus (115ii–iv) are all interrogatives. (115iii–iv) form a special subclass of interrogatives, since they are formed by the additional subsidiary transformation T_w. Thus when we formulate the simplest transformational grammar for (115), we find that the intuitively correct classification of sentences is given by the resulting transformational representations.

9

SYNTAX AND SEMANTICS

9.1 We have now found cases of sentences that are understood in more than one way and are ambiguously represented on the transformational level (though not on other levels) and cases of sentences that are understood in a similar manner and are similarly represented on the transformational level alone. This gives an independent justification and motivation for description of language in terms of transformational structure, and for the establishment of transformational representation as a linguistic level with the same fundamental character as other levels. Furthermore it adds force to the suggestion that the process of "understanding a sentence" can be explained in part in terms of the notion of linguistic level. In particular, in order to understand a sentence it is necessary to know the kernel sentences from which it originates (more precisely, the terminal strings underlying these kernel sentences) and the phrase structure of each of these elementary components, as well as the transformational history of development of the given sentence from these kernel sentences.[1] The general problem of analyzing the process of "understanding" is thus reduced, in a sense, to the problem of explaining how kernel sentences are understood, these being considered the basic 'content elements' from which the usual, more complex sentences of real life are formed by transformational development.

---

[1] When transformational analysis is more carefully formulated, we find that knowledge of the transformational representation of a sentence (which incorporates the phrase structure of the kernel strings from which the sentence originates) is all that is necessary to determine the derived phrase structure of the transform.

In proposing that syntactic structure can provide a certain insight into problems of meaning and understanding we have entered onto dangerous ground. There is no aspect of linguistic study more subject to confusion and more in need of clear and careful formulation than that which deals with the points of connection between syntax and semantics. The real question that should be asked is: "How are the syntactic devices available in a given language put to work in the actual use of this language?" Instead of being concerned with this very important problem, however, the study of interconnections between syntax and semantics has largely been dominated by a side issue and a misformulated question. The issue has been whether or not semantic information is required for discovering or selecting a grammar; and the challenge usually posed by those who take the affirmative in this dispute is: "How can you construct a grammar with no appeal to meaning?"

The remarks in § 8 about possible semantic implications of syntactic study should not be misinterpreted as indicating support for the notion that grammar is based on meaning. In fact, the theory outlined in §§ 3–7 was completely formal and non-semantic. In § 8, we have indicated briefly some ways in which the actual use of available syntactic devices can be studied. Perhaps this problem can be elucidated somewhat further by a purely negative discussion of the possibility of finding semantic foundations for syntactic theory

9.2.1 A great deal of effort has been expended in attempting to answer the question: "How can you construct a grammar with no appeal to meaning?" The question itself, however, is wrongly put, since the implication that obviously one can construct a grammar *with* appeal to meaning is totally unsupported. One might with equal justification ask: "How can you construct a grammar with no knowledge of the hair color of speakers?" The question that should be raised is: "How can you construct a grammar?" I am not acquainted with any detailed attempt to develop the theory of grammatical structure in partially semantic terms or any specific and rigorous proposal for the use of semantic information in constructing or evaluating grammars. It is undeniable that "intuition about linguistic form" is very useful to the investigator of linguistic form (i.e., grammar). It is also quite clear that the major goal of grammatical theory is to replace this obscure reliance on intuition by some rigorous and objective approach. There is, however, little evidence that "intuition about meaning" is at all useful in the actual investigation of linguistic form. I believe that the inadequacy of suggestions about the use of meaning in grammatical analysis fails to be apparent only because of their vagueness and because of an unfortunate tendency to confuse "intuition about linguistic form" with "intuition about meaning," two terms that have in common only their vagueness and their undesirability in linguistic theory. However, because of the widespread acceptance of such suggestion, it may be worthwhile to investigate some of them briefly, even though the burden of proof in this case rests completely on the linguist who claims to have been able to develop some grammatical notion in semantic terms.

9.2.2 Among the more common assertions put forth as supporting the dependence of grammar on meaning we have the following:

(117) (i)   two utterances are phonemically distinct if and only if they differ in meaning;

(ii)   morphemes are the smallest elements that have meaning;

(iii)   grammatical sentences are those that have semantic significance;

(iv)   the grammatical relation subject-verb (i.e., $NP - VP$ as an analysis of *Sentence*) corresponds to the general 'structural meaning' actor-action;

(v)   the grammatical relation verb-object (i.e., $Verb - NP$ as an analysis of VP) corresponds to the structural meaning action-goal or action-object of action;

(vi)   an active sentence and the corresponding passive are synonymous.

9.2.3 A great many linguists have expressed the opinion that phonemic distinctness must be defined in terms of differential meaning (synonymity, to use a more familiar term), as proposed in

(117i). However, it is immediately evident that (117i) cannot be accepted, as it stands, as a definition of phonemic distinctness.[2] If we are not to beg the question, the utterances in question must be tokens, not types. But there are utterance tokens that are phonemically distinct and identical in meaning (synonyms) and there are utterance tokens that are phonemically identical and different in meaning (homonyms). Hence (117i) is false in both directions. From left to right it is falsified by such pairs as "bachelor" and "unmarried man," or, even more seriously, by such absolute synonyms as /ekɪnámiks/ and /iykɪnámiks/ ("economics"), "ádult" and "adúlt," /rǽšɪn/ and /réyšɪn/, ("ration"), and many others, which may coexist even within one style of speech. From right to left, (117i) is falsified by such pairs as "bank" (of a river) and "bank" (for savings),[3] "metal" and "medal" (in many dialects), and numerous other examples. In other words, if we assign two utterance tokens to the same utterance type on the basis of (117i), we will simply get the wrong classification in a large number of cases.

A weaker claim than (117i) might be advanced as follows. Suppose that we have an absolute phonetic system given in advance of the analysis of any language, and guaranteed to be detailed enough so that every two phonemically distinct utterances in any language will be differently transcribed. It may now be the case that certain different tokens will be identically transcribed in this phonetic transcription. Suppose that we define the "ambiguous meaning" of an utterance token as the set of meanings of all tokens transcribed identically with this utterance token. We might now revise (117i), replacing "meaning" by "ambiguous meaning." This might provide an approach to the homonymity problem, if we had an immense corpus in which we could be fairly sure that each of the

---

[2] See my "Semantic considerations in grammar," *Monograph no. 8*, pp. 141–53 (1955), for a more detailed investigation of (117i).

[3] Note that we cannot argue that "bank" in "the river bank" and "bank" in "the savings bank" are two occurrences of the same word, since this is precisely the question under investigation. To say that two utterance tokens are occurrences of the same word is to say that they are not phonemically distinct, and presumably this is what the synonymity criterion (117i) is supposed to determine for us.

phonetically distinct forms of a given word occurred with each of the meanings that this word might have. It may be possible to elaboratei this approach even further to cope with the problem cf synonyms. In such a way one might hope to determine phonemo distinctness by laborious investigation of the meanings of phonetic-allytranscribed items in a vast corpus. The difficulty of determining in any precise and realistic manner how many meanings several items may have in common, however, as well as the vastness of the undertaking, make the prospect for any such approach appear rather dubious.

9.2.4 Fortunately, we do not have to pursue any such far-fetched and elaborate program in order to determine phonemic distinctness. In practice, every linguist uses much more simple and straight-forward non-semantic devices. Suppose that a linguist is interested in determining whether or not "metal" and "medal" are phonemic-ally distinct in some dialect of English. He will not investigate the meanings of these words, since this information is clearly irrelevant to his purpose. He knows that the meanings are different (or he is simply not concerned with the question) and he is interested in determining whether or not the words are phonemically distinct. A careful field worker would probably use the pair test,[4] either with two informants or with an informant and a tape recorder. For example, he might make a random sequence of copies of the utterance tokens that interest him, and then determine whether or not the speaker can consistently identify them. If there is consistent identification, the linguists may apply an even stricter test, asking the speaker to repeat each word several times, and running the pair test over again on the repetitions. If consistent distinguishability is maintained under repetition, he will say that the words "metal" and "medal" are phonemically distinct. The pair test with its variants

---

[4] Cf. my "Semantic considerations of grammar," *Monograph no. 8*, pp. 141–54 (1955); M. Halle, "The strategy of phonemics," *Linguistics Today, Word* 10.197–209 (1954); Z. S. Harris, *Methods in structural linguistics* (Chicago, 1951), pp. 32f.; C. F. Hockett, *A manual of phonology* = *Memoir 11, Indiana University Publications in Anthropology and Linguistics* (Baltimore, 1955), p. 146.

and elaborations provides us with a clear operational criterion for phonemic distinctness in completely non-semantic terms.[5]

It is customary to view non-semantic approaches to grammar as possible alternatives to semantic approaches, and to criticize them as too complex, even if possible in principle. We have found, however, that in the case of phonemic distinctness, at least, exactly the opposite is true. There is a fairly straightforward and operational approach to the determination of phonemic distinctness in terms of such non-semantic devices as the pair test. It may be possible in principle to develop some semantically oriented equivalent to the pair test and its elaborations, but it appears that any such procedure will be quite complex, requiring exhaustive analysis of an immense corpus, and involving the linguists in the rather hopeless attempt to determine how many meanings a given phone sequence might have.

---

[5] Lounsbury argues in his "A semantic analysis of the Pawnee kinship usage," *Language* 32.158–94 (1956), p. 190, that appeal to synonymity is necessary to distinguish between free variation and contrast: "If a linguist who knows no English records from my lips the word *cat* first with a final aspirated stop and later with a final preglottalized unreleased stop, the phonetic data will not tell him whether these forms contrast or not. It is only when he asks me, his informant, whether the meaning of the first form is different from that of the second, and I say it is not, that he will be able to proceed with his phonemic analysis." As a general method, this approach is untenable. Suppose that the linguist records /ekɪnamiks/ and /iykɪnamiks/, /viksɪn/ and /fiymeyl ⧧ faks/, etc., and asks whether or not they are different in meaning. He will learn that they are not, and will incorrectly assign them the same phonemic analysis, if he takes this position literally. On the other hand, there are many speakers who do not distinguish "metal" from "medal," though if asked, they may be quite sure that they do. The responses of such informants to Lounsbury's direct question about meaning would no doubt simply becloud the issue.

We can make Lounsbury's position more acceptable by replacing the question "do they have the same meaning?" with "are they the same word?" This will avoid the pitfalls of the essentially irrelevant semantic question, but it is hardly acceptable in this form, since it amounts to asking the informant to do the linguist's work; it replaces an operational test of behavior (such as the pair test) by an informant's judgment about his behavior. The operational tests for linguistic notions may require the informant to respond, but not to express his opinion about his behavior, his judgment about synonymy, about phonemic distinctness, etc. The informant's opinions may be based on all sorts of irrelevant factors. This is an important distinction that must be carefully observed if the operational basis for grammar is not be trivialized.

9.2.5   There is one further difficulty of principle that should be mentioned in the discussion of any semantic approach to phonemic distinctness. We have not asked whether the meanings assigned to distinct (but phonemically identical) tokens are identical, or merely very similar. If the latter, then all of the difficulties of determining phonemic distinctness are paralleled (and magnified, because of the inherent obscurity of the subject matter) in determining sameness of meaning. We will have to determine when two distinct meanings are sufficiently similar to be considered 'the same.' If, on the other hand, we try to maintain the position that the meanings assigned are always identical, that the meaning of a word is a fixed and unchanging component of each occurrence, then a charge of circularity seems warranted. It seems that the only way to uphold such a position would be to conceive of the meaning of a token as "the way in which tokens of this type are (or can be) used," the class of situations in which they can be used, the type of response that they normally evoke, or something of this sort. But it is difficult to make any sense at all out of such a conception of meaning without a prior notion of utterance type. It would appear, then, that even apart from our earlier objections, any approach to phonemic distinctness in semantic terms is either circular or is based on a distinction that is considerably more difficult to establish than the distinction it is supposed to clarify.

9.2.6   How, then, can we account for the widespread acceptance of some such formulation as (117i)? I think that there are two explanations for this. In part, it is a consequence of the assumption that semantic approaches are somehow immediately given and are too simple to require analysis. Any attempt to provide a careful description, however, quickly dispels this illusion. A semantic approach to some grammatical notion requires as careful and detailed a development as is justly required of any non-semantic approach. And as we have seen, a semantic approach to phonemic distinctness is beset by quite considerable difficulties.

A second source for such formulations as (117i), I believe, is a confusion of "meaning" with "informant's response." We thus find such comments on linguistic method as the following: "In linguistic analysis we define contrast among forms operationally in terms of difference in meaning responses."[6] We have observed in § 9.2.3 that if we were to determine contrast by 'meaning response' in any direct way we would simply make the wrong decision in a great many places; and if we try to avoid the difficulties that immediately arise, we are led to a construction that is so elaborate and has such intolerable assumptions that it can be hardly taken as a serious proposal. And we saw in § 9.2.5 that there are apparently even more fundamental difficulties of principle. Hence, if we interpret the quoted assertion literally, we must reject it as incorrect.

If we drop the word "meaning" from this statement, however, we have a perfectly acceptable reference to such devices as the pair test. But there is no warrant for interpreting the responses studied in the pair test as semantic in any way.[7] One might very well develop an operational test for rhyme that would show that "bill" and "pill" are related in a way in which "bill" and "ball" are not. There would be nothing semantic in this test. Phonemic identity is essentially complete rhyme, and there is no more reason for postulating some unobserved semantic reaction in the case of "bill" and "bill" than in the case of "bill" and "pill."

It is strange that those who have objected to basing linguisitc theory on such formulations as (117i) should have been accused of disregard for meaning. It appears to be the case, on the contrary, that those who propose some variant of (117i) must be interpreting "meaning" so broadly that any response to language is called "meaning." But to accept this view is to denude the term "meaning" of any interest or significance. I think that anyone who wishes to save the phrase "study of meaning" as descriptive of an important

---

[6] F. Lounsbury, "A semantic analysis of the Pawnee kinship usage", *Language* 32.158–94 (1956), p. 191.

[7] One should not be confused by the fact that the subject in the pair test may be asked to identify the utterance tokens by meaning. He might just as well be asked to identify them by arbitrarily chosen numbers, by signs of the zodiac, etc. We can no more use some particular formulation of the pair test as an argument for dependence of grammatical theory on meaning than as an argument that linguistics is based on arithmetic or astrology.

aspect of linguistic research must reject this identification of "meaning" with "response to language," and along with it, such formulations as (117 i).

9.2.7 It is, of course, impossible to prove that semantic notions are of no use in grammar, just as it is impossible to prove the irrelevance of any other given set of notions. Investigation of such proposals, however, invariably seems to lead to the conclusion that only a purely formal basis can provide a firm and productive foundation for the construction of grammatical theory. Detailed investigation of each semantically oriented proposal would go beyond the bounds of this study, and would be rather pointless, but we can mention briefly some of the more obvious counterexamples to such familiar suggestion as (117).

Such morphemes as "to" in "I want to go" or the dummy carrier "do" in "did he come?" (cf. § 7.1) can hardly be said to have a meaning in any independent sense, and it seems reasonable to assume that an independent notion of meaning, if clearly given, may assign meaning of some sort to such non-morphemes as *gl-* in "gleam," "glimmer," "glow."[8] Thus we have counterexamples to the suggestion (117 ii) that morphemes be defined as minimal meaning-bearing elements. In § 2 we have given grounds for rejecting "semantic significance" as a general criterion for grammaticalness, as proposed in (117 iii). Such sentences as "John received a letter" or "the fighting stopped" show clearly the untenability of the assertion (117 iv) that the grammatical relation subject-verb has the 'structural meaning' actor-action, if meaning is taken seriously as a concept independent of grammar. Similarly, the assignment (117 v) of any such structural meaning as action-goal to the verb-object relation as such is precluded by such sentences as "I will disregard his incompetence" or "I missed the train." In contradiction to (117 vi), we can describe circumstances in which a 'quantificational' sentence such as "everyone in the room knows at

---

[8] See L. Bloomfield, *Language* (New York, 1933), p. 156; Z. S. Harris, *Methods in structural linguistics* (Chicago, 1951), p. 177; O. Jespersen, *Language* (New York, 1922), chapter XX, for many further examples.

least two languages" may be true, while the corresponding passive
"at least two languages are known by everyone in the room" is false,
under the normal interpretation of these sentences — e.g., if one
person in the room knows only French and German, and another
only Spanish and Italian. This indicates that not even the weakest
semantic relation (factual equivalence) holds in general between
active and passive.

9.3   These counterexamples should not, however, blind us to the
fact that there are striking correspondences between the structures
and elements that are discovered in formal, grammatical analysis
and specific semantic functions. None of the assertions of (117)
is wholly false; some are very nearly true. It seems clear, then, that
undeniable, though only imperfect correspondences hold between
formal and semantic features in language. The fact that the correspondences are so inexact suggests that meaning will be relatively
useless as a basis for grammatical description.[9] Careful analysis of
each proposal for reliance on meaning confirms this, and shows, in
fact, that important insights and generalizations about linguistic
structure may be missed if vague semantic clues are followed too
closely. For example, we have seen that the active-passive relation
is just one instance of a very general and fundamental aspect of
formal linguistic structure. The similarity between active-passive,
negation, declarative-interrogative, and other transformational
relations would not have come to light if the active-passive relation
had been investigated exclusively in terms of such notions as
synonymity.

[9]   Another reason for suspecting that grammar cannot be effectively developed on a semantic basis was brought out in the particular case of phonemic
distinctness in § 9.2.5. More generally, it seems that the study of meaning is
fraught with so many difficulties even after the linguistic meaningbearing
elements and their relations are specified, that any attempt to study meaning
independently of such specification is out of the question. To put it differently,
given the instrument language and its formal devices, we can and should investigate their semantic function (as, e.g., in R. Jakobson, "Beitrag zur allgemeinen Kasuslehre," *Travaux du Cercle Linguistique de Prague* 6.240–88
(1936)); but we cannot, apparently, find semantic absolutes, known in advance
of grammar, that can be used to determine the objects of grammar in any way.

The fact that correspondences between formal and semantic features exist, however, cannot be ignored. These correspondences should be studied in some more general theory of language that will include a theory of linguistic form and a theory of the use of language as subparts. In § 8 we found that there are, apparently, fairly general types of relations between these two domains that deserve more intensive study. Having determined the syntactic structure of the language, we can study the way in which this syntactic structure is put to use in the actual functioning of language. An investigation of the semantic function of level structure, as suggested briefly in § 8, might be a reasonable step towards a theory of the interconnections between syntax and semantics. In fact, we pointed out in § 8 that the correlations between the form and use of language can even provide certain rough criteria of adequacy for a linguistic theory and the grammars to which it leads. We can judge formal theories in terms of their ability to explain and clarify a variety of facts about the way in which sentences are used and understood. In other words, we should like the syntactic framework of the language that is isolated and exhibited by the grammar to be able to support semantic description, and we shall naturally rate more highly a theory of formal structure that leads to grammars that meet this requirement more fully.

Phrase structure and transformational structure appear to provide the major syntactic devices available in language for organization and expression of content. The grammar of a given language must show how these abstract structures are actually realized in the case of the language in question, while linguistic theory must seek to clarify these foundations for grammar and the methods for evaluating and choosing between proposed grammars.

It is important to recognize that by introducing such considerations as those of § 8 into the metatheory that deals with grammar and semantics and their points of connection, we have not altered the purely formal character of the theory of grammatical structure itself. In §§ 3-7 we outlined the development of some fundamental linguistic concepts in purely formal terms. We considered the problem of syntactic research to be that of constructing a device for producing a given set of grammatical sentences and of studying the properties of grammars that do this effectively. Such semantic notions as reference, significance, and synonymity played no role in the discussion. The outlined theory, of course, had serious gaps in it — in particular, the assumption that the set of grammatical sentences is given in advance is clearly too strong, and the notion of "simplicity" to which appeal was made explicitly or tacitly was left unanalyzed. However, neither these nor other gaps in this development of grammatical theory can be filled in or narrowed, to my knowledge, by constructing this theory on a partially semantic basis.

In §§ 3–7, then, we were studying language as an instrument or a tool, attempting to describe its structure with no explicit reference to the way in which this instrument is put to use. The motivation for this self-imposed formality requirement for grammars is quite simple — there seems to be no other basis that will yield a rigorous, effective, and 'revealing' theory of linguistic structure. The requirement that this theory shall be a completely formal discipline is perfectly compatible with the desire to formulate it in such a way as to have suggestive and significant interconnections with a parallel semantic theory. What we have pointed out in § 8 is that this formal study of the structure of language as an instrument may be expected to provide insight into the actual use of language, i.e., into the process of understanding sentences.

9.4   To understand a sentence we must know much more than the analysis of this sentence on each linguistic level. We must also know the reference and meaning[10] of the morphemes or words of

---

[10]   Goodman has argued—to my mind, quite convincingly—that the notion of meaning of words can at least in part be reduced to that of reference of expressions containing these words. See N. Goodman, "On likeness of meaning," *Analysis*, vol. 10, no. 1 (1949); idem, "On some differences about meaning," *Analysis*, vol. 13, no. 4 (1953). Goodman's approach amounts to reformulating a part of the theory of meaning in the much clearer terms of the theory of reference, just as much of our discussion can be understood as suggesting a reformulation of parts of the theory of meaning that deal with so-called "structural meaning" in terms of the completely nonsemantic theory of grammatical structure. Part of the difficulty with the theory of meaning is that "meaning"

which it is composed; naturally, grammar cannot be expected to be of much help here. These notions form the subject matter for semantics. In describing the meaning of a word it is often expedient, or necessary, to refer to the syntactic framework in which this word is usually embedded; e.g., in describing the meaning of "hit" we would no doubt describe the agent and object of the action in terms of the notions "subject" and "object", which are apparently best analyzed as purely formal notions belonging to the theory of grammar.[11] We shall naturally find that a great many words or morphemes of a single grammatical category are described semantically in partially similar terms, e.g. verbs in terms of subject and object, etc. This is not surprising; it means that the syntactic devices available in the language are being used fairly systematically. We have seen, however, that so generalize from this fairly systematic use and to assign 'structural meanings' to grammatical categories or constructions just as 'lexical meanings' are assigned to words or morphemes, is a step of very questionable validity.

Another common but dubious use of the notion 'structural meaning' is with reference to the meanings of so-called 'grammatically functioning' morphemes such as *ing*, *ly*, prepositions, etc. The contention that the meanings of these morphemes are fundamentally different from the meanings of nouns, verbs, adjectives, and perhaps other large classes, is often supported by appeal to the fact that these morphemes can be distributed in a sequence of blanks or nonsense syllables so as to give the whole the appearance of a sentence, and in fact, so as to determine the grammatical category of the nonsense elements. For example, in the sequence "Pirots karulize etalically" we know that the three words are noun, verb, and adverb by virtue of the *s*, *ize*, and *ly*, respectively. But this

---

tends to be used as a catch-all term to include every aspect of language that we know very little about. Insofar as this is correct, we can expect various aspects of this theory to be claimed by other approaches to language in the course of their development.

[11] Such a description of the meaning of "hit" would then account automatically for the use of "hit" in such transforms as "Bill was hit by John," "hitting Bill was wrong," etc., if we can show in sufficient detail and generality that transforms are 'understood' in terms of the underlying kernel sentences.

property does not sharply distinguish 'grammatical' morphemes from others, since in such sequences as "the Pirots karul — yesterday" or "give him — water" the blanks are also determined as a variant of past tense, in the first case, and as "the", "some," etc., but not "a," in the second. The fact that in these cases we were forced to give blanks rather than nonsense words is explained by the productivity or 'open-endedness' of the categories Noun, Verb, Adjective, etc., as opposed to the categories Article, Verbal Affix, etc. In general, when we distribute a sequence of morphemes in a sequence of blanks we limit the choice of elements that can be placed in the unfilled positions to form a grammatical sentence. Whatever differences there are among morphemes with respect to this property are apparently better explained in terms of such grammatical notions as productivity, freedom of combination, and size of substitution class than in terms of any presumed feature of meaning.

10

SUMMARY

In this discussion we have stressed the following points: The most that can reasonably be expected of linguistic theory is that it shall provide an evaluation procedure for grammars. The theory of linguistic structure must be distinguished clearly from a manual of helpful procedures for the discovery of grammars, although such a manual will no doubt draw upon the results of linguistic theory, and the attempt to develop such a manual will probably (as it has in the past) contribute substantially to the formation of linguistic theory. If this viewpoint is adopted, there is little motivation for the objection to mixing levels, for the conception of higher-level elements as being literally constructed out of lower-level elements, or for the feeling that syntactic work is premature until all problems of phonemics or morphology are solved.

Grammar is best formulated as a self-contained study independent of semantics. In particular, the notion of grammaticalness cannot be identified with meaningfulness (nor does it have any special relation, even approximate, to the notion of statistical order of approximation). In carrying out this independent and formal study, we find that a simple model of language as a finite state Markov process that produces sentences from left to right is not acceptable, and that such fairly abstract linguistic levels as phrase structure and transformational structure are required for the description of natural languages.

We can greatly simplify the description of English and gain new and important insight into its formal structure if we limit the direct description in terms of phrase structure to a kernel of basic sentences (simple, declarative, active, with no complex verb or noun phrases), deriving all other sentences from these (more properly, from the strings that underlie them) by transformation, possibly repeated. Conversely, having found a set of transformations that carry grammatical sentences into grammatical sentences, we can determine the constituent structure of particular sentences by investigating their behavior under these transformations with alternative constituent analyses.

We consequently view grammars as having a tripartite structure. A grammar has a sequence of rules from which phrase structure can be reconstructed and a sequence of morphophonemic rules that convert strings of morphemes into strings of phonemes. Connecting these sequences, there is a sequence of transformational rules that carry strings with phrase structure into new strings to which the morphophonemic rules can apply. The phrase structure and morphophonemic rules are elementary in a sense in which the transformational rules are not. To apply a transformation to a string, we must know some of the history of derivation of this string; but to apply non-transformational rules, it is sufficient to know the shape of the string to which the rule applies.

As an automatic consequence of the attempt to construct the simplest grammar for English in terms of the abstract levels developed in linguistic theory we find that the apparently irregular behavior of certain words (e.g., "have," "be," "seem") is really a case of higher level regularity. We also find that many sentences are assigned dual representations on some level, and many pairs of sentences are assigned similar or identical representations on some level. In a significant number of cases, dual representation (constructional homonymity) corresponds to ambiguity of the represented sentence and similar or identical representation appears in cases of intuitive similarity of utterances.

More generally, it appears that the notion of "understanding a sentence" must be partially analyzed in grammatical terms. To understand a sentence it is necessary (though not, of course, sufficient) to reconstruct its representation on each level, including the transformational level where the kernel sentences underlying a given sentence can be thought of, in a sense, as the 'elementary content elements' out of which this sentence is constructed. In other words, one result of the formal study of grammatical structure is that a syntactic framework is brought to light which can support semantic analysis. Description of meaning can profitably refer to this underlying syntactic framework, although systematic semantic considerations are apparently not helpful in determining it in the first place. The notion of "structual meaning" as opposed to "lexical meaning", however, appears to be quite suspect, and it is questionable that the grammatical devices available in language are used consistently enough so that meaning can be assigned to them directly. Nevertheless, we do find many important correlations, quite naturally, between syntactic structure and meaning; or, to put it differently, we find that the grammatical devices are used quite systematically. These correlations could form part of the subject matter for a more general theory of language concerned with syntax and semantics and their points of connection.

11

Appendix I

NOTATIONS AND TERMINOLOGY

In this appendix we shall present a brief account of the new or less familiar notational and terminological conventions that we have used.

A linguistic level is a method of representing utterances. It has a finite *vocabulary* of symbols (on the phonemic level, we call this vocabulary the *alphabet* of the language) which can be placed in a linear sequence to form *strings* of symbols by an operation called *concatenation* and symbolized by + Thus on the morphemic level in English we have the vocabulary elements *the, boy, S, past, come,* etc., and we can form the string *the + boy + S + come + past* (which would be carried by the morphophonemic rules into the string of elements /ðɨbɔ́yz ǂ kéym./) representing the utterance "the boys came." Apart form the phonemic level, we have used italics or quotes for vocabulary symbols and strings of representing symbols; on the phonemic level we suppress the concatenation symbol + and use the customary slant lines, as in the example just given. We use *X, Y, Z, W* as variables over strings.

Occasionally we use a hyphen instead of the plus sign, to symbolize concatenation. We do this to call special attention to a subdivision of the utterance with which we happen to be particularly concerned at the moment. Sometimes we use wider spacing for the same purpose. Neither of these notational devices has any systematic significance; they are introduced simply for clarity in exposition. In the discussion of transformations, we use the hyphen

(118) $NP - have - en + V$ (cf. (37iii))

inverting the first two segments, we mean that it applies, for example, to

(119)   *they − have − en + arrive.*

since *they* is an *NP* and *arrive* is a *V* in this string. The transform in this case will be

(120)   *have − they − en + arrive,*

ultimately, "have they arrived?"

A rule of the form $X \rightarrow Y$ is to be interpreted as the instruction "rewrite X as Y," where X and Y are strings. We use parentheses to indicate that an element may or may not occur, and brackets (or listing) to indicate choice among elements. Thus both the rules (121i) and (121ii)

(121) (i) $a \rightarrow b$ (c)

(ii) $a \rightarrow \begin{Bmatrix} b + c \\ b \end{Bmatrix}$

are abbreviations for the pair of alternatives: $a \rightarrow b + c$, $a \rightarrow b$.

The following list gives the page references for the first occurrence of the special symbols other than those mentioned above.

(122)

NP	p. 26	S	p. 39
VP	p. 26	$\emptyset$	p. 39
T	p. 26	*past*	p. 39
N	p. 26	*Af*	p. 39
NP_{sing}	p. 28	$\#$	p. 39
NP_{pl}	p. 29	A	p. 65
$[\Sigma, F]$	p. 29	*wh*	p. 69, fn. 2
Aux	p. 39	*Adj*	p. 72
V	p. 39	*PP*	p. 74
C	p. 39	*Prt*	p. 75
M	p. 39	*Comp*	p. 76
en	p. 39		

12

Appendix II

EXAMPLES OF ENGLISH PHRASE STRUCTURE AND TRANSFORMATIONAL RULES

We collect here for ease of reference the examples of rules of English grammar that played an important role in the discussion. The numbers to the left give the proper ordering of these rules, assuming that this sketch is the outline of a grammar of the form (35). The parenthesized number to the right of each rule is the number of this rule in the text. Certain rules have been modified from their forms in the text in the light of subsequent decision or for more systematic presentation.

Phrase Structure:

Σ: # *Sentence* #

F:	1.	$Sentence \rightarrow NP + VP$	(13 i)
	2.	$VP \rightarrow Verb + NP$	(13 iii)
	3.	$NP \rightarrow \begin{cases} NP_{sing} \\ NP_{pl} \end{cases}$	(p. 29, fn. 3)
	4.	$NP_{sing} \rightarrow T + N + \emptyset$	(p. 29, fn. 3)
	5.	$NP_{pl} \rightarrow T + N + S$	(p. 29, fn. 3)
	6.	$T \rightarrow the$	(13 iv)
	7.	$N \rightarrow man, ball, etc.$	(13 v)
	8.	$Verb \rightarrow Aux + V$	(28 i)
	9.	$V \rightarrow hit, take, walk, read, etc.$	(28 ii)
	10.	$Aux \rightarrow C(M) (have + en) (be + ing)$	(28 iii)
	11.	$M \rightarrow will, can, may, shall, must$	(28 iv)

Transformational Structure:

A transformation is defined by the structural analysis of the strings to which it applies and the structural change that it effects on these strings.

12. *Passive* – optional:

Structural analysis: $NP - Aux - V - NP$

Structural change: $X_1 - X_2 - X_3 - X_4 \rightarrow X_4 - X_2 + be +$
$en - X_3 - by + X_1$ (34)

13. T^{ob}_{sep} – obligatory:

Structural analysis: $\begin{cases} X - V_1 - Prt - Pronoun \\ X - V_2 - Comp - NP \end{cases}$ (86)
    (92)

Structural change: $X_1 - X_2 - X_3 - X_4 \rightarrow X_1 - X_2 - X_4 - X_3$

14. T^{op}_{sep} – optional:

Structural analysis: $X - V_1 - Prt - NP$ (85)

Structural change: same as 13

15. *Number Transformation* – obligatory

Structural analysis: $X - C - Y$

Structural change: $C \rightarrow \begin{cases} S \text{ in the context } NP_{sing} - \\ \varnothing \text{ in other contexts} \\ past \text{ in any context} \end{cases}$ (29i)

16. T_{not} – optional

Structural analysis: $\begin{cases} NP - C - V \ldots \\ NP - C + M - \ldots \\ NP - C + have - \ldots \\ NP - C + be - \ldots \end{cases}$ (37)

Structural change: $X_1 - X_2 - X_3 \rightarrow X_1 - X_2 + n't - X_3$

17. T_A – optional:

Structural analysis: same as 16   (cf. (45)–(47))

Structural change: $X_1 - X_2 - X_3 \rightarrow X_1 - X_2 + A - X_3$

18. T_q – optional:

Structural analysis: same as 16   (cf. (41)–(43))

Structural change: $X_1 - X_2 - X_3 \rightarrow X_2 - X_1 - X_3$

19. T_w – optional and conditional on T_q:

T_{w1}: Structural analysis: $X - NP - Y$ (X or Y may be null)

Structural change: same as 18   (60i)

T_{w2}: Structural analysis: $NP - X$ (60ii)

Structural change: $X_1 - X_2 \rightarrow wh + X_1 - X_2$

where $wh +$ animate noun $\rightarrow who$ (cf. p. 69, fn. 2)

$wh +$ animate noun $\rightarrow what$

20. *Auxiliary Transformation* — obligatory:
Structural analysis: $X - Af - v - Y$ (where Af is any C or is
en or *ing*; v is any M or
V, or *have* or *be*) (29 ii)
Structural change: $X_1 - X_2 - X_3 - X_4 \rightarrow X_1 - X_3 - X_2 \# - X_4$

21. *Word Boundary Transformation* — obligatory:
Structural analysis: $X - Y$ (where $X \ddagger v$ or $Y \ddagger Af$) (29 iii)
Structural change: $X_1 - X_2 \rightarrow X_1 - \# X_2$

21. *do — Transformation* — obligatory:
Structural analysis: $\# - Af$ (40)
Structural change: $X_1 - X_2 \rightarrow X_1 - do + X_2$

Generalized Transformations:

22. Conjunction (26)
Structural analysis: of S_1: $Z - X - W$
of S_2: $Z - X - W$
where X is a minimal element (e.g., *NP*, *VP*, etc.) and
Z, W are segments of terminal strings.
Structural change: $(X_1 - X_2 - X_3; X_4 - X_5 - X_6) \rightarrow X_1 -$
$X_2 + and + X_5 - X_3$

23. T_{so}: (48)–(50)
Structural analysis: of S_1: same as 16
of S_2: same as 16
Structural change: $(X_1 - X_2 - X_3; X_4 - X_5 - X_6) \rightarrow$
$X_1 - X_2 - X_3 - and - so - X_5 - X_4$
T_{so} is actually a compound with the conjunction transformation.

24. Nominalizing Transformation T_{to}: (p. 72, fn. 3)
Structural analysis: of S_1: $NP - VP$
of S_2: $X - NP - Y$ (X or Y may be null)
Structural change: $(X_1 - X_2; X_3 - X_4 - X_5) \rightarrow X_3 - to +$
$X_2 - X_5$

25. Nominalizing Transformation T_{ing}: (p. 72, fn. 3)
Same as 24, with *ing* in place of *to* in Structural change

26. Nominalizing Transformation T_{Adj}:   (71)
Structural analysis: of S_1: $T - N - is - A$
of S_2: same as 24
Structural change: $(X_1 - X_2 - X_3 - X_4; X_5 - X_6 - X_7) \rightarrow$
$X_5 - X_1 + X_4 + X_2 - X_7$

Morphophonemic Structure:

Rules (19); (45); p. 58, fn. 8; p. 69, fn. 2; etc.

We thus have three sets of rules, as in (35): rules of phrase structure, transformational rules (including simple and generalized transformations), and morphophonemic rules. Order of rules is essential, and in a properly formulated grammar it would be indicated in all three sections, along with a distinction between optional and obligatory rules and, at least in the transformational part, a statement of conditional dependence among rules. The result of applying all of these rules is an extended derivation (such as (13)–(30)–(31)) terminating in a string of phonemes of the language under analysis, i.e., a grammatical utterance. This formulation of the transformational rules is meant only to be suggestive. We have not developed the machinery for presenting all these rules in a proper and uniform manner. See the references cited in fn. 8, p. 44, for a more detailed development and application of transformational analysis.

BIBLIOGRAPHY

1. Y. Bar-Hillel, "Logical syntax and semantics," *Language* 30.230–7 (1954).
2. B. Bloch, "A set of postulates for phonemic analysis," *Language* 24.3–46 (1948).
3. L. Bloomfield, *Language* (New York, 1933).
4. N. Chomsky, *The logical structure of linguistic theory* (mimeographed).
5. ——, "Semantic considerations in grammar," *Monograph no. 8*, pp. 141–53 (1955), The Institute of Languages and Linguistics, Georgetown University.
6. ——, "Systems of syntactic analysis," *Journal of Symbolic Logic* 18.242–56 (1953).
7. ——, "Three models for the description of language," *I.R.E.Transactions on Information Theory*, vol. IT-2, Proceedings of the symposium on information theory, Sept., 1956.
8. ——, *Transformational analysis*, Ph. D. Dissertation, University of Pennsylvania (1955).
9. ——, with M. Halle and F. Lukoff, "On accent and juncture in English," *For Roman Jakobson* ('s-Gravenhage, 1956).
10. M. Fowler, Review of Z. S. Harris, *Methods in structural linguistics*, in *Language* 28.504–9 (1952).
11. N. Goodman, *The structure of appearance* (Cambridge, 1951).
12. ——, "On likeness of meaning," *Analysis*, vol. 10, no. 1 (1949).
13. ——, "On some differences about meaning," *Analysis*, vol. 13, no. 4 (1953). Both 12 and 13 are reprinted, with an additional note, in *Philosophy and Analysis*, M. Macdonald, editor (New York, 1954).
14. M. Halle, "The strategy of phonemics," *Linguistics Today*, *Word* 10.197–209 (1954).
15. Z. S. Harris, "Discourse analysis," *Language* 28.1–30 (1952).
16. ——, "Distributional structure," *Linguistics Today*, *Word* 10.146–62 (1954).
17. ——, "From phoneme to morpheme," *Language* 31.190–222 (1955).
18. ——, *Methods in structural linguistics* (Chicago, 1951).
19. ——, "Cooccurrence and transformations in linguistic structure," *Language* 33. 283–340 (1957).
20. F. W. Harwood, "Axiomatic syntax; the construction and evaluation of a syntactic calculus," *Language* 31.409–14 (1955).
21. L. Hjelmslev, *Prolegomena to a theory of language* = *Memoir 7, Indiana Publications in Anthropology and Linguistics* (Baltimore, 1953).
22. C. F. Hockett, "A formal statement of morphemic analysis," *Studies in Linguistics* 10.27–39 (1952).

116 BIBLIOGRAPHY

23. ——, *A manual of phonology* = *Memoir 11, Indiana University Publications in Anthropology and Linguistics* (Baltimore, 1955).
24. ——, "Problems of morphemic analysis," *Language* 23.321–43 (1947).
25. ——, "Two models of grammatical description," *Linguistics Today, Word* 10.210–33 (1954).
26. ——, "Two fundamental problems in phonemics," *Studies in Linguistics* 7.33 (1949).
27. R. Jakobson, "Beitrag zur allgemeinen Kasuslehre," *Travaux du Cercle Linguistique de Prague* 6.240–88 (1936).
28. ——, "The phonemic and grammatical aspects of language and their interrelation," *Proceedings of the Sixth International Congress of Linguists* 5–18 (Paris, 1948).
29. O. Jespersen, *Language* (New York, 1922).
30. F. Lounsbury, "A semantic analysis of the Pawnee kinship usage," *Language* 32.158–94 (1956).
31. B. Mandelbrot, "Simple games of strategy occurring in communication through natural languages," *Transactions of the I.R.E.*, Professional Group on Information Theory, PGIT-3, 124–37 (1954).
32. ——, "Structure formelle des textes et communication: deux études," *Word* 10.1–27 (1954).
33. E. Nida, *A synopsis of English syntax* (South Pasadena, 1951).
34. K. L. Pike, "Grammatical prerequisites to phonemic analysis," *Word* 3.155–72 (1947).
35. ——, "More on grammatical prerequisites," *Word* 8.106–21 (1952).
36. W. V. Quine, *From a logical point of view* (Cambridge, 1953).
37. C. E. Shannon and W. Weaver, *The mathematical theory of communication* (Urbana, 1949).
38. H. A. Simon, "On a class of skew distribution functions," *Biometrika* 42.425–40 (1955).
39. R. S. Wells, "Immediate constituents," *Language* 23.81–117 (1947).

SOME ADDITIONAL BIBLIOGRAPHY ON
GENERATIVE GRAMMAR

Bar-Hillel, Y., C. Gaifman, E. Shamir, "On categorial and phrase-structure grammars", *The Bulletin of the Research Council of Israel*, vol. 9F, 1–16 (1960).
Bar-Hillel, Y., M. Perles, E. Shamir, *On formal properties of simple phrase structure grammars*, Technical report no. 4, U.S. Office of Naval Research, Information Systems Branch (July, 1960).
Chomsky, N., "A transformational approach to syntax", *Proceedings of the 1958 University of Texas Symposium on Syntax* (to appear).
——, "On certain formal properties of grammars", *Information and Control* 2.133–67 (1959).
——, "A note on phrase structure grammars", *Information and Control* 2.393–5 (1959).
——, "On the notion 'rule of grammar'", *Proceedings of the symposium on the structure of language and its mathematical aspects*, American Mathematical Society, vol. 12.6–24 (1961).

——, "Some methodological remarks on generative grammar", *Word* 17. 219–239 (1961).

——, "Explanatory models in Linguistics", *Proceedings of the 1960 International Congress on Logic, Methodology and Philosophy of Science*, P. Suppes, editor, (to appear).

Chomsky, N., and M. Halle, *The sound pattern of English* (to appear).

Gleitman, L., "Pronominals and Stress in English Conjunctions" (to appear in *Language Learning*).

——, "Causative and Instrumental Structures in English" (to appear).

Halle, M., *The sound pattern of Russian* ('s-Gravenhage, 1959).

——, "Questions of linguistics", *Nuovo Cimento* 13.494–517 (1959).

——, "On the role of simplicity in linguistic descriptions", *Proceedings of the symposium on the structure of language and its mathematical aspects*, American Mathematical Society, vol. 12.89–94 (1961).

Halle, M., and K. Stevens, "Analysis by synthesis", in: L. E. Woods and W. Wathen-Dunn, eds., *Proceedings of the Seminar on Speech Compression and Processing*, Dec. 1959, AFCRC-TR-'59–198, vol II, paper D–7.

Householder, F., "On linguistic primes", *Word* 15 (1959).

Klima, E. S., "Negation in English" (to appear).

Lees, R. B., *The grammar of English nominalizations*, Supplement to *International Journal of American Linguistics* 26 (1960).

——, "A multiply ambiguous adjectival construction in English", *Language* 36.207–221 (1960).

——, "The English comparative construction", *Word* 17.171–185 (1961).

——, "O pereformulirovanii transformacionnyx grammatik" (to appear in *Voprosy Jazykoznanija 10 # 6* (1961)).

——, "On the So-called 'Substitution-in-Frames' Technique" (to appear in *General Linguistics*).

——, "On the Constituent-Structure of English Noun-Phrases" (to appear in *American Speech*).

——, "Some Neglected Aspects of Parsing" (to appear in *Language Learning*).

——, "The Grammatical Basis of Some Semantic Notions" (to appear in *Proceedings of the Eleventh Annual Round Table Conference*, Georgetown University Monograph Series).

——, "On the Testability of Linguistic Predicates" (to appear in *Voprosy Jazykoznanija 11* (1962)).

——, *Turkish Phonology* (to be published by *Uralic and Altaic Series*, Indiana University (1962)).

——, "A Compact Analysis for the Turkish Personal Morphemes" (to appear in *American Studies in Altaic Linguistics*, Indiana University, (1962)).

Matthews, G. H., "On Tone in Crow", *IJAL* 25.135–6 (1959).

——, "A grammar of Hidatsa" (to appear).

——, "Analysis by synthesis of sentences of natural languages", *Proceedings of the International Conference on Mechanical Translation and Applied Linguistics*, National Physical Laboratory, Teddington.

Smith, C. S., "A class of complex modifiers in English" (to appear in *Language*).

Stockwell, R. P., "The place of intonation in a generative grammar of English", *Language* 36 (1960).